Praise for *Little Stone Lion*

"Combining skillful storytelling with powerful, practical wisdom, Susanna encourages us to use creativity and innovation to reimagine the business landscape. Little Stone Lion is a powerful guidebook for those committed to leading with purpose and compassion, achieving financial success and nurturing our planet and its resources".
— Marci Shimoff, #1 New York Times bestselling author, renowned speaker, California

"If you seek wisdom over knowledge, this read is for you. Allow yourself to be transported to experiences of the soul."
— Ida Abdalkhani, International Speaker & Award-Winning CEO, Global Board Member of Women Presidents' Organization

"Susanna Qiang Huang's book "Little Stone Lion" stands as a beacon of graceful simplicity in the realm of business literature. Seamlessly weaving together Eastern and Western philosophies, this book invites readers to delve deeply into various business functions while offering a panoramic view of the business landscape. Like an artist meticulously painting a small bird that embodies the majesty of a giant eagle, Huang captures both the intricate details and the magical power of the interconnectedness of business operations."

Written with eloquence and poetic charm, "Little Stone Lion" is enriched with pearls of wisdom drawn from Huang's own entrepreneurial journey. Through authentic and inspirational stories, Huang not only educates but also inspires readers to explore purpose-driven business practices that pursue lasting happiness and benefit our Mother Earth.

This book transcends business strategy; it is a celebration of creativity, innovation, and sustainability. Huang's narrative encourages readers to reimagine traditional business frameworks and offers profound insights that resonate long after the final page. For aspiring entrepreneurs and business students alike, "Little Stone

Lion" is a compelling read that illuminates the path to entrepreneurial success with clarity, wisdom, and a heartfelt commitment to making a meaningful impact."

— Professor Zhi-Long Chen, Dean's Chair in Management Science Robert H. Smith School of Business, University of Maryland, USA

"I have known Susanna for the last two decades, observing her professional journey from working for large corporations to running a start-up, as well as the enjoyment she derived from the journey. This book has benefited from her vast business experiences and her unique understanding of both Western and Eastern business cultures. It provides a great business framework that can be applied to practical business problems both holistically and systematically. It is an excellent combination of management theory and real-world business practices."

— Song Qi, Executive Vice President of a Global Fortune 500 manufacturer and an MBA alumnus of Ohio Fisher College of Business.

"Little Stone Lion," deftly crafted by Susanna, unravels the complexities of business through an extraordinary blend of elegance, simplicity, and penetrating insight. Each sentence, radiant and potent, guides the reader through the intricate labyrinth of entrepreneurship, offering an immersive Zen journey. We accompany Susanna in her quest to expand her knowledge by sharing it, a testament to her belief in mutual growth. The book breathes life into the principles she champions, seamlessly marrying profitability with purpose and harmonizing intellectual depth with emotional resonance. At its core, "Little Stone Lion" serves as a luminous beacon of holistic, purposeful entrepreneurship - an indispensable read for those bold visionaries intent on making a lasting impact."

— Jan Rippingale, Founder, CEO, Thought Leader & Keynote Speaker in Solar Industry, California

"This unique book offers an innovative exploration of how Zen principles can be applied to the business world. The author intertwines Zen philosophy with modern business strategies, creating a unique perspective on entrepreneurship and leadership that are rooted in the author's own journey and her poetic personal reflections in each chapter such as "Business is also an Art. A great brand is a masterpiece of Art…" that is so beautifully and artistically rendered in words. This book is particularly insightful for those interested in how mindfulness and spiritual values can enhance business practices, decision-making, and brand building. It's a narrative that weaves business acumen with a spiritual, minimalist approach, ideal for those seeking a holistic view of entrepreneurship and business strategy."

— Dr. Xuhui Shao, Former VP of Yahoo, Managing Partner of Tech VC, Silicon Valley, CA, USA

"Little Stone Lion is a breath of fresh air in a world of constant uncertainty. Implementing Susanna's ideas to go zen, and go green, can help one to live in the present and stay focused on what matters most. We all have so much to give to the planet, and this book can help you get there!"

— Tyler Kanczuzewski, VP of Sustainability, reGen South Bend, Indiana

"I especially enjoyed the coda, "Little Stone Lion: The End". It weaves together the personal, the philosophical, and the practical aspects of her journey as a green entrepreneur, as a minority, a woman, an immigrant, and an underdog. I feel the encouragement, unity, and empowerment, and it is quite inviting for readers like me to embark on our own transformative journeys."

— Zhaoyang "Leon" Liang, Zhaoyang Liang, VP Executive, Global Financial Services, Arizona, USA

Susanna is a courageous, resilient Chinese woman with a touch of romanticism. She not only pursues excellence in her endeavors but also maintains a reflective mindset, consistently using her writing to capture the truth. I believe this work will inspire and nourish you through her stories."

— Jiehui Liu, Renowned Writer and Publisher in Beijing, China

"Little Stone Lion" elevates beyond the typical scope of management literature. As I delved into its chapters, it felt like engaging in a deep, meaningful conversation with a long-missed friend, accompanied by the gentle comfort of floral tea. Here, I was captivated by her open recounting of entrepreneurial tales, interspersed with challenges and victories, introspective thoughts, and the luminous pearls of wisdom. Susanna's prose is concise yet vibrant, abundantly insightful yet remarkably approachable, all woven together with a touch of graceful refinement."

— Daniel Leung, OSU Fisher MBA Alumni Board Member, Consultant, Hongkong

"Susanna's storytelling and practical wisdom inspire us to use creativity and innovation in business. "Little Stone Lion" is a guide for leading with purpose, achieving financial success, and caring for our planet."

— Frank Agin, Founder and President of AmSpirit Business Connections, Ohio

"Susanna's sincere words, I see the story of a hardworking entrepreneur's transformation into a successful leader, from a puzzled practitioner following the flow to a confident industry leader who has found her true self. I hope you can join me in gaining multifaceted inspiration from this work, both in business and in personal growth and values. Furthermore, I hope her positive energy and sparkling light will bring starlight to more lives and make our shared world a better place."

— Hui Zhang, Executive, Global Logistics Companies, Texas, USA

"As an entrepreneur, I am deeply drawn to the author's Zen-inspired infusion thinking. Infusion is the key to resolving conflicts and achieving visions; it is the embodiment of long-termism. The author's multinational experiences and cross-disciplinary perspectives constantly flow with the poetry, positive energy, and mindfulness that infusion brings. On the path of entrepreneurship, especially at crossroads, this book will certainly lead you into a state of flow, helping you realize your own business Zen essence."

— Dr. Bo Guan, Founder and CEO of High Tech Company in China

A solar Wechat friend I have net met, sent Lao Hong an electronic copy of the book Little Stone Lion, wanting to know Lao Hong's thoughts after reading it. At first, I simply skimmed through it, worried that I might shy away from such language, as it's not something I encounter every day. But unexpectedly, Little Stone Lion not only introduced me to a different kind of language, but also opened up a whole new world where I met Susanna Huang (月溪, Moon Creek), a person from this other world.

It's astonishing that someone can use poetic language to explain philosophy, Zen, business, and solar technologies, blending thoughts, career, and life into a quiet flowing river from their hands. Here, the solar panels you touch are not cold; they are warm. Here, solar panels are no longer just objects but become a form of solace, filling people with imagination.

A person who can inspire others to dream must first be filled with dreams themselves. But not every dreamer has the courage to act on their dreams. Susanna is someone who dares to dream and dares to act.

In 2011, after learning the ideas of solar technology and business sustainability, Susanna resolutely left a Fortune 500 company to tell the entrepreneurial story of a green consulting company. Five years later, the company began collaborating with world-renowned enterprises, and ten years later, it won a prestigious brand award in the solar industry.

In Lao Hong's view, romance and business are contradictory—romance is warmth, and business is cold. But Susanna has perfectly combined romance and business, becoming a successful romantic entrepreneur. However, what Lao Hong sees as Susanna greatest success is not how much money was earned, but rather the achievement of installing the company's inverters on the Eiffel Tower, making it shine brightly with solar power.

— Wei Hong, Chief Solar Industry Researcher in China

"Numerous business managers have regarded books like 'Jack: Straight from the Gut' and 'The Essays of Warren Buffett' as essential guides for learning about business strategy and management in the US market. After decades of personal experience working in multinational businesses, my longing to read a book authored by a China-US business expert, with a specific focus on Chinese companies engaged in global and US market operations, has grown immensely. For managers at all levels, this book "Little Stone Lion" serves as your comprehensive guide to advancing your business within both the US and the international market. And for all business owners, this book is highly recommended if your company isn't prepared for a million-dollar consultancy project yet still seeks invaluable insights."

— Edward Yu, Sr. Executive in Solar Industry, MBA from the University of Hull, UK

"Little Stone Lion" is a compelling and insightful read, especially for small business owners navigating the competitive landscape. One of the standout aspects of the book is its focus on the mindset and resilience required to thrive against larger competitors. It offers a fresh perspective on the entrepreneurial journey, emphasizing that success is not solely about size or resources but about vision, determination, and the ability to adapt."

— Grant Carpenter, Associate Attorney in Columbus Ohio USA

"Susanna is an exceptionally talented and respected Chinese woman, as well as an outstanding writer. Her writing is elegant and refined, with a keen insight into life. Reading her work is a delightful experience, and it is well worth your time."

— Mengji Li, Renowned Writer, Million Copies Sold

"Combining skillfull storytelling with powerful, pratical wisdom"
Marci Shimoff, #1 New York Times bestselling author

Little Stone Lion

Go Global. In Zen. In Green.

Susanna Qiang Huang

Little Stone Lion

Qiang Huang

Copyright © Susanna Qiang Huang 2025

Published by 1st World Publishing
P.O. Box 2211, Fairfield, Iowa 52556
tel: 641-209-5000 ♦ fax: 866-440-5234
web: www.1stworldpublishing.com

First Edition

ISBN: 978-1-4218-3567-9

LCCN: Library of Congress Cataloging-in-Publication Data

All rights reserved. Printed in the United States of America. No part of this book may be used or reproduced in any manner whatsoever without written permission except in the case of brief quotations embodied in critical articles and reviews.

Table of Contents

Preface: Little Stone Lion 15
The Eiffel Tower Has a "Noble Heart" 17
A Small Bird Flies in the Sunshine 21
Go Global. In Zen. In Green. 25
For A Brand, Flower is Flower, Tree is Tree 31
    Brand Building in Every Action 33
    Ultra-Simple Zen-Inspired Brand 35
    Sacred Soul Seed 37
    Growth in All Seasons 39
    Great Brands – Monet's Water Lilies 41
    Peak Emotions, Deeply Touching 43
    Tarnished Brand, Revitalized. 45
Great Products Shine a Brand's Light 49
    Thinking Like Top Customers 53
        Product Design for Service. 55
        Product Design for Supply Chain 57
        Product Design for Marketing 59
    Standards, Not Stacks of Papers. 60
    Products Tests via Third-Party. 62
    Product Quality, Invisible to the Eye 64
    Product Roadmaps for the Future 66
Service is Sales, in Enso Circles. 69
    Service as Sales, Not 2nd Sales. 73
        Business Selling Service 74
        Service Keeping Sales. 75
        Sales Coming from Service. 76
    Service Trends 77
        Self-Service 77
        Artificial Intelligence for Service. 77
        Service Automation 78
        Customized Service Solutions 78

"SOAK" in Service, Best-in-Class 80
    S – Self-Service 80
    O – Outsource 80
    A – Automation 81
    K – Knowledge base 82
Service Smarter in "ABC" 84
    A – Artificial Intelligence (AI) 84
    B – Business Intelligence 84
    C – Circle of Intelligence 84
Training as Service, Unexpected 85
    Marketing Alternative 85
    Sales Lead Generation 85
    Customer Training 86
Sell Values with Courage 89
    Business Partnership vs. Transactions 92
    Thinking Like Big Customers 94
    Many-to-Many Collaborations 97
    A Fresh Sales Perspective 99
Marketing is Attraction 103
    Marketing Aligned with Brand 107
        Rooted in Brand Essence 108
        Peak Emotions Captured 108
        Various Marketing Channels 109
    Enso's Social Media Solar System 110
        Contents Created with Ease 111
    Different Brand Phases 114
        Germination Phase: Led by Dreams 114
        Early Phase: Driven by Businesses 114
        Explosive Growth Phase: Loved by Consumers 115
        Decline Phase: Creating from Nothingness 116
Organizations are Like Water 119
    "PACKS" Organization Strategy 123
        P – Process Mapping 123
        A – Accountability Assignment 124
        C – Cross-Functional Team 125
        K – KPI Measurement 126
        S – Share Knowledge 128

"ADDED" Dynamic Projects 130
   A – Assemble Team 131
   D – Define Objectives 132
   D – Diversify Ideas 132
   E – Execute with Freedom 132
   D – Deliver and Share 133
Build Trust: Reliability in "PCS" 134
   P – Product Reliability 135
   C – Company Reliability 135
   S – Service Reliability 136
Harmonious Operational Systems 137
Strategic Sourcing, Supplier Collaborations 139
7 Reasons for Insourcing from Outsourcing 143
   Reason 1: Core Business Operations 144
   Reason 2: Cost Considerations 144
   Reason 3: Collaboration Challenges 144
   Reason 4: Ethical Concerns 145
   Reason 5: Evolving Business Requirements 145
   Reason 6: Clouded Communications 145
   Reason 7: Trusting Your Gut Feelings 146
Personal Transformation is a Business Strategy 149
   7 Most Important Questions 153
   7 Common Learning Mistakes to Avoid 156
      Mistake #1: No Longer Learning Proactively 157
      Mistake #2: Not Having a Guide for Education 158
      Mistake #3: Not Knowing One's Own Genius 159
      Mistake #4: Not Getting Fresh Knowledge 160
      Mistake #5: Not Mastering Soft Skills 161
      Mistake #6: Not Nurturing or Supporting Community 162
      Mistake #7: Not Having a Higher Purpose 163
   Read and Write 165
   Chasing Knowledge like "CATS" 167
      C – Create Knowledge 168
      A – Apply Knowledge 168
      T – Teach Knowledge 169
      S – Share Knowledge 169
   Wonderful Passions 170

- Minority and Introvert? So Be It. 172
- Poetry, Beyond Passion 174
- Calm and Joyful at Meru Peak 176
- Unity in Human Communities, A Return to Paris 178

7 Stars Global Solar Education Guide 181
- B.E.S.T. Are for Stars 185
  - B – Business: Unleash Your Potentials 187
  - E – Equipment: Unveil Soul of Business 190
  - S – Standards: Unleash Power of Compliance 193
  - T – Transformation: Embrace Your Journey. 195
  - A – Applications: Unlock the Power. 197
  - F – Financing: Unlock the Potential of Solar Energy . . 199
  - S – Services: Creating Delightful Customer Experiences 201

Business is Art, in Zen Simplicity. 205
- A Poem About Starbucks Bears 207
- "PRICE" Flows, Be Water. 208
  - P – Product Flow. 209
  - R – Reverse Product Flow 209
  - I – Information Flow. 210
  - C – Cash Flow. 211
  - E – Energy Flow 212

"U & I": The New Rules of Business 215
- U – Uniqueness. 217
- I – Interconnectedness. 217

Little Stone Lion: The End. 221

About the Author: Rising from Nothingness 225

Acknowledgement 230

For my Dear Father, Junxing Huang,

Your love always warms my heart.

Preface: Little Stone Lion

A ray of golden morning light
shines upon the little stone lion

He once lost his way in dark nights
But never lost his dreams
to explore the unknown land

He waits
until a ray of morning light
shines upon him

— "Moon Creek" Poetry

The Eiffel Tower Has a "Noble Heart"

"It is technology married with liberal arts, married with the humanities, that yields the results that make our hearts sing."

— Steve Jobs

As night fell, I found myself sitting on stone steps, gazing at the majestic Eiffel Tower in the distance.

I was captivated by the slowly radiating golden light of the Eiffel Tower in the dark night.

It was the summer of 2014, and I was exploring Paris on foot.

The visitor counts at the International Renewable Energy Exhibition in Paris had dropped significantly, but it did not dampen my spirits to tour the city.

The following year, in 2015, I received an email from our New York installer, informing me that they had installed our inverters on the Eiffel Tower.

I wrote an article, "Reaching for the Sky", published in the *North American Clean Energy* magazine.

As I wrote this chapter, it dawned on me that the Paris Agreement was also adopted in 2015.

At the center of the Paris Agreement poster stands the Eiffel Tower, gently touching people's hearts.

Two seemingly unrelated dots connected in my mind in a flash.

When the Eiffel Tower was endowed with a new "heart", a renewable energy system, it found a new purpose in its precious life, inspiring people to Go Global, In Green.

Technologies are only the tools we use.

The overarching aim of humankind is to seek happiness, both in life and in business.

Technologies may be cold. The hearts of we, humans, are warm energy fields, filled with love and compassion, that can be felt by people over mountains, across seas, and through Time and Space.

A Small Bird Flies in the Sunshine

"Business is a soul-awakening journey, not just a money-accumulation journey."

– Susanna Huang

Walking toward the security gate inside the Columbus International Airport, my attention was attracted to the big overhead billboard. A small and lovely bird was being projected by the light as the shadow of a big eagle.

This image resonated deeply within me. Green Energy Village, my boutique management consulting business, founded in Dublin, was that small and lovely bird.

In 2011, I left Mettler Toledo, a Fortune 500 global manufacturer, where I learned about solar energy and sustainability at our week-long global management training program in the tranquil scenery of Switzerland.

I decided to take on the new solar industry, attracted by the magic it promised.

I started with only a laptop and a vision, in the Starbucks Café inside our local Barnes and Noble bookstore.

A decade later, our woman-owned and minority-owned small business was named in the Top 10 Solar Energy Technologies Consulting Services Companies. We also won the prestigious EuPD Top Brand PV Inverter Award in the United States, the only one in our niche market, beating other business giants—the big eagles.

We are now living in a new world, facing unknowns and uncertainties.

Remember the mass extinctions of dinosaurs? Big businesses now face similar big adaption challenges.

I observed that getting smaller is a mega business trend in this post-pandemic world, as small businesses may have a much better chance to survive.

But small is not enough, small businesses must be graceful and powerful, like this small and lovely bird.

Or be like a young David, who defeated Giant Goliath.

Green Energy Village is living proof.

Go Global. In Zen. In Green.

"Small and Graceful Business Blooms in the Zen Garden of Ultra-Simplicity."

– Susanna Huang

This business book is written to stand out as a beacon of graceful simplicity within business literature, seamlessly weaving together Eastern and Western philosophies.

It invites readers to delve deeply into various business functions while offering a bird's-eye view of the business landscape. Like an artist meticulously painting a small and lovely bird that embodies the majesty of a giant eagle, this book captures both the intricate details and the magical power of business interconnectedness.

This book transcends business strategy; it is a celebration of creativity, innovation, and sustainability.

I combine the imaginative application of management consulting from my Accenture experience with the creative use of management tools employed by large companies, and the systematic application of analytical thinking developed through my rigorous electrical engineering education.

Written with poetic, lyrical language, *Little Stone Lion* is enriched with pearls of wisdom handpicked from the scenic creek of my entrepreneurial journey.

Through authentic and inspirational stories, this book not only educates but also inspires readers to explore purpose-driven business practices that pursue lasting happiness and benefit Mother Earth.

The *Little Stone Lion* business book is tailored to resonate with a broad audience at different stages of their entrepreneurial journey.

Management consultants seeking fresh strategic perspectives will find forward-thinking strategies.

Established business owners will discover innovative strategies to refresh their business approaches and integrate sustainable practices.

Corporate escapees looking to transition into entrepreneurship will find invaluable insights.

Business students, especially those in entrepreneurship programs, will gain a holistic view of business that melds Western management with Eastern wisdom.

Aspiring entrepreneurs will find inspiration and practical advice, helping them navigate the early stages of setting up their businesses.

Early-stage startups can leverage the book's framework to build a solid foundation and sidestep common pitfalls.

Advocates of green energy and sustainability will appreciate the book's commitment to environmental principles, facing climate change challenges.

Additionally, Zen and mindfulness practitioners will benefit from the integration of Zen principles into business practices.

Minority and women business owners, as well as global thinkers operating across international markets, will find the cross-cultural insights and diverse perspectives especially compelling.

After reading this book, You will crystallize your assumptions and reimagine your business visions.

You will build your own Enso's Inner House of Business Framework holistically.

You will design unique strategies for each business function, systematically and coherently.

You will achieve ultimate simplicity and cost-effectiveness in business operations with the Zen spirit.

You will unlock your true business potential and build a solid foundation for your great business growth.

*

Since everyone is familiar with a house, below, I use the metaphor of a house to illustrate Enso's Inner House of Business Framework.

	Enso's Inner House of Business Framework	
	Foundation	Brand
	Roof	Organization
	Pillar 1	Product
	Pillar 2	Sales
	Pillar 3	Service
	Pillar 4	Marketing
	Garden	Personal Transformation
	Illustrator: Katie Lu	

For A Brand, Flower is Flower, Tree is Tree

> "Brand is Everything We Do in Business, Starting from Day One."
>
> – Susanna Huang

Let's start with Brand, our house's foundation, although many people often prioritize other aspects of the business.

Brand Building in Every Action

It was my first exhibition at Solar Power International, the largest solar trade show in North America.

I found myself alone assembling our booth at the last minute, as my colleague could not come due to an unforeseeable reason. It was a time-consuming task, and by the time I'd finished, it was already late into the night. As I looked around the vast and empty exhibition hall, fear crept in. However, the next morning brought a renewed sense of hope as the exhibition hall filled with beautiful booths and numerous visitors.

But very few people stopped by our booth. After all, why would they come to visit an unknown brand?

Starting my boutique management consulting business, I aspired to build a top solar brand from day one, with nothing but a laptop and a vision. It was a humble start.

There are two common assumptions that entrepreneurs often make about brand:

First, they believe that making money for survival should take precedence over brand, and second, they perceive growing a brand as a costly endeavor that requires significant time and resources.

However, as an entrepreneur, I've come to a different realization:

Brand is everything we do in business.

Brand is significant, setting the tone for the business, and influencing various business functions such as product offerings, sales strategies, service provision, marketing approaches, organizational development, and personal growth.

Years later, our dedication and efforts were recognized. Luck was on our side in 2015 when we partnered with renowned solar companies such as SolarCity/Tesla, Sunrun, Flex, and IUSA. Later, we were awarded the prestigious top brand awards, despite being the little bird among the big eagle solar industry giants.

My strategy of cultivating a Zen-inspired Solar Brand, from day one, came to fruition.

In the following chapters, I will delve deeper into this unique brand strategy and illustrate how it may transform your business.

Ultra-Simple Zen-Inspired Brand

Steve Jobs went to India in his younger years, but his guru had passed away by the time Jobs arrived. However, this exploration of Eastern spirituality greatly impacted his philosophy and approach to business and life. Steve Jobs practiced Zen Meditation ever since. He was known for his magical "reality distortion field."

In Webster's dictionary, Zen is a state of calm attentiveness in which one's actions are guided by intuition rather than by conscious effort.

One day, as I walked through serene woods, surrounded by the symphony of birds and the graceful leaps of deer, a profound realization dawned upon me.

In the state of Zen Meditation, I have come to comprehend the Brand Essence:

A great brand grows much like a majestic tree from its soul seed.

It is fitting to draw an analogy between these natural wonders and our brands.

Just as a tiny flower seed transforms into a fragrant flower, or a humble sapling grows into a mighty oak, a brand too follows a similar path. An oak tree bathes in the warm embrace of sunlight, while a pine tree dons a majestic aura under the shimmering moonlight. Each seed holds its potential to become a unique manifestation of nature's beauty.

My own decade-long Zen Meditation practice along my solar adventure was like embarking on a magical internal journey, not a direct path, but moving in the circles of self-discovery, until some day I may reach its center, my true self, in emptiness, with my crystal-clear life purpose.

If we could identify our life purpose, visualizing our goals as the distant peaks of the Himalaya Mountains, we could walk toward it with confidence, with minimum detours, and wasting few earth resources.

Often, we find ourselves expending valuable time, resources, and energy in attempting to transform a flower into a tree, or a tree into a flower.

My solar entrepreneurship journey leads me to believe that it is truly possible to build a purpose-driven business while establishing a great brand with lean operations, in both large and small businesses.

Embrace the power of ultra-simplicity Zen-inspired brand and let your brand flourish like a resilient seed, transforming into an extraordinary presence in the business world.

Sacred Soul Seed

"Dream Your Business and Manifest It in Reality."

– Susanna Huang

I initially endeavored to mold myself in the image of my dad, an engineer turned successful entrepreneur, and other entrepreneurs with engineering backgrounds. Yet, I found myself discontented, unfulfilled, and unsuccessful. I was a flower, wanting to grow into a tree, and it was not working.

I took a big, long detour in my pursuit of entrepreneurship and growing our brand.

It was only when I discovered who I am, accepted who I am, and accepted my uniqueness, even if it made me uncomfortable, that I found my true calling and success. I embraced the graceful fusion of art and technology born within me, akin to the harmonious blend found in the magnificence of the Eiffel Tower.

Deep within each of us resides a unique and precious soul seed, waiting to be unveiled.

This sacred seed holds the potential to cultivate a truly magnificent business brand.

Take, for instance, the legendary "Apple Tree" that blossomed from the soul seed of Steve Jobs. These extraordinary entrepreneurs often discover their inherent uniqueness at a tender age, nurturing it to fruition throughout their remarkable journeys.

It took years for me to realize that it is not only acceptable but empowering to embrace our uniqueness and differences. By embracing our distinctiveness, we release the potential to build a unique brand, graceful and powerful, with resounding success.

A great brand germinates when its founder awakens to ponder the fundamental questions of human existence:

"Who am I?"

"What is my life purpose on Mother Earth?"

In that precious transformative moment, a founder catches a glimpse of their own soul seed, igniting the spark of profound realization within.

My boutique management consulting business brand is my creation of poetry in business, exquisite and succinct, inspired by Zen Meditation, and created and nurtured on a profound journey of self-discovery.

Growth in All Seasons

Over the last decade in the solar industry, I've seen many shooting stars falling pitifully into dark nights.

Several world-leading solar manufacturers have seen their glory fade or vanish entirely.

Once number one in the world, a prominent German solar inverter brand, for instance, lost most of its residential market share within just a year, due to the introduction of new industry standards and regulations.

A leading California-based solar inverter brand experienced a rapid decline in its market presence following persistent quality issues, and was later acquired by a leading European brand.

An Israeli brand that initially dominated about 80% of the residential solar market saw its fortunes plummet after its legendary founder sadly passed away.

Nature, in all its wisdom, mirrors the essence of entrepreneurship.

Amidst the woods, many seeds fail to survive or thrive, buffeted by strong winds, drenched by pouring rains, and shrouded in winter's icy grasp. Some, however, survive, precious seeds that strive to grow in solitude and darkness.

Yet, in nurturing environments, these seeds may one day grow into magnificent trees. An oak tree dons a beautiful robe of golden leaves in the autumn, while its branches stand bare in the cold of winter.

A great brand thrives in all business environments, steadfastly embodying the soul of its founder.

Witnessing the journey of a great brand unfold is akin to witnessing the awakening of its founder.

Over a tumultuous decade in the solar industry, our business remained steadfast in the game, whether the skies were sunny or overcast. We consistently showcased our presence at major solar trade shows and maintained a resilient local team. We learned valuable lessons, rebounded from setbacks, and evolved through self-discovery.

Amidst these challenges, I sought solace in reading and writing, often in the tranquility of the natural scenery in Moon Creek. I dedicated myself to personal transformation as an entrepreneur first, shouldering the entirety of my business responsibilities in all seasons. When opportunities presented themselves, I met them with enthusiasm and embarked on new ventures.

Like the resilient trees that dance harmoniously with the wind, we, as entrepreneurs, also navigate the ebb and flow of business, ensuring growth while protecting us from risks. By aligning ourselves with the natural rhythms of entrepreneurship, we nurture our brands to flourish.

Great Brands – Monet's Water Lilies

"Business is also an Art. A great brand is a masterpiece of Art."

– Susanna Huang

Standing before Monet's water lilies in the New York Metropolitan Museum of Art, I marvelled at the intricate brushstrokes that at first glance appear random. Yet, as I stepped back and gazed from afar, I was captivated by the ethereal beauty of water lilies adrift in a misty pond.

Forgetting the individual strokes, I was touched by the emotion of love Monet poured into his art. Monet spent countless hours observing the ever-changing light dancing upon the water lilies, day and night, months and years, painting what touched his heart subtlety and deeply. And even now, his paintings continue to light up our souls.

A great entrepreneur is akin to an accomplished artist, first painting the masterpiece of enterprise in the mind, then meticulously crafting it stroke by stroke in business, just as Monet brought his water lilies to life. The activities of the business are orchestrated, and the products and services are delivered with a unique rhythm that's harmonious with the soul of its founder from day one.

A great brand encompasses everything, emanating from the very essence of its founder, with the same aura.

A business organization is, in essence, an extension of the founder's identity, embodying the same purpose, vision and values that first ignited its creation.

Our solar business is genuinely unique, shaped by a series of Zen-inspired decisions made over days and nights spanning a decade. Each of these decisions is akin to a brushstroke gracefully applied to a masterpiece of art.

For example, our product remains elegantly simple, akin to plain vanilla ice cream, avoiding unnecessary complexity. We intentionally engage top-tier customers, diligently navigating their requirements and meeting their stringent standards. Our marketing strategy revolves around solar education for the masses, with minimal reliance on traditional marketing investments. Service excellence is underpinned by a custom-designed, world-class CRM platform, enabling us to achieve more with less, leveraging the power of digital transformation. Our team members are cross-functional, multi-talented, and brimming with creativity. Our lean organization emphasizes agility and efficiency. Lastly, our brand has been meticulously crafted through long-term interactions with solar installers.

A great brand grows in tandem with the personal transformation of its founder, who peers into their own reflection, seeking to reconnect with authentic self and life purpose time and again. This introspective journey ensures that the great brand remains true to its unique essence, the precious soul seed, illuminating a golden glow amidst a sea of conformity.

Peak Emotions, Deeply Touching

"It is only with the heart that one can see rightly; what is essential is invisible to the eye."

– Little Prince

One day, I received a message, informing me that the marketing director was laughing at the short service videos I had recently asked our product engineers to produce. Later, these videos were widely viewed by solar installers nationwide, with one receiving over 60,000 views without any 3rd party marketing promotions—nearly 100 times more than the number of views of similar expensive professional videos.

Contrary to popular belief, a great brand is not merely a collection of words inked on fine paper, nor is it solely comprised of impressive images adorning a glossy brochure or captivating videos shared on social media. No, it transcends these superficial aspects.

A brand has the power to evoke unparalleled emotions in its customers. These emotions reach a peak, setting it apart from ordinary brands. The peak emotions a brand stirs are unique and authentic experiences that touch the people's hearts, akin to a masterpiece of art.

True brand success lies beyond superficial elements. It lies in the sensibility to identify and understand the peak emotions that resonate with the target audience, like Monet's waterlilies.

Our product engineer solved the problems for these solar installers with pure intentions to help, talking to them using their languages in these short service videos, as he was one of them. People trusted him.

The task of a great business is to capture these peak emotions, infusing them into every aspect of the business and communicating them through strategic marketing messages to audiences.

This understanding becomes the cornerstone of a highly effective marketing program, providing a solid foundation for building a well-respected brand, with minimum marketing investments.

Tarnished Brand, Revitalized

"Feel the Aura of a Business."

– Susanna Huang

I had a 360-degree business experience that spans start-up and established businesses.

I made an intriguing observation: the illuminating auras surrounding some businesses lose their glow over time. The stock prices of such public companies also drop dramatically.

In this regard, I would like to shed light on three key reasons behind this phenomenon and share how to revitalize the original illuminating aura.

First and foremost, founders often get lost amidst the chaotic world of business. They may become blinded by the allure of success or overwhelmed by the challenges they face, dampening their inner light. To revitalize the business aura, the founder must embark on an inner journey of self-discovery, reconnecting with their inner light radiating from their souls.

Second, the individuals surrounding the founders may unknowingly misalign themselves with the purposes, visions, and missions of the businesses. Their own auras inadvertently cloud the business aura. The founders have the responsibilities to guide people in a unified direction, much like a school of small fish swimming together, resembling a large magnificent fish.

Lastly, there may be a few individuals within the business who fabricate the aura by mimicking the founder's radiance, all while concealing their self-serving activities. By keenly observing with the mind's eyes, the founder can detect the subtle odor veiled secretly beneath, just as one can distinguish between a fragrance and a strong scent. To restore the business aura to its former illuminating glow, the founder must remove the fabricated elements or distance themselves swiftly.

Great Products Shine a Brand's Light

"Feel the Product is to Feel the Essence of Its Business."

– Susanna Huang

Sitting on a bus transporting people to a huge solar exhibition hall, a young man asked me to visit his business booth. I said yes. Why not? It was the beginning of my solar adventure. I didn't know many people yet.

Walking past the crowd, I found the tranquil booth, which looked like it was floating in the clouds. The white inverter products sat next to the white sofa, an elegance that's rarely seen in the marketing of industrial products. I liked the aura and quickly decided to work with this company, though I only met one person, the sales manager.

It was a good decision. This company became my largest management consulting client for over a decade, growing more than 20 times its original size, and rising from an unknown brand to a top 3 global inverter brand and a public company.

In the initial years of our entrepreneurial journey together, our exhibition booths attracted few visitors, our products garnered little to no interest, and our sales revenues were small.

Several years ago, quality issues plagued the solar inverter products of several leading global manufacturers, leading them to withdraw from the United States. The local market suffered from significant after-sales service problems, with replacement parts being frequently unavailable, and damages to users' solar system earnings. The emerging solar industry's reputation was in jeopardy.

Top banks and major clients became extremely cautious, initiating global strategic sourcing initiatives to look for new solar inverter business partners, similar to my strategic sourcing projects for Fortune 500 companies. The once tightly shut doors of the United States solar market finally opened a narrow crack, and we encountered a rare and invaluable business opportunity. We grabbed it firmly, a small, little-known brand.

Many businesses' problems stem from people's subconscious self-imposed limitations. If you start by telling yourself that something is impossible, it often becomes that way. However, I saw our huge potential.

I successfully connected with SolarCity, Sunrun, and VivintSolar, the top three residential solar installers in the United States. Convincing them to allow us to participate in the inverter supplier evaluation was a challenging task. The three major clients subjected us to a series of rigorous factory inspections and evaluations of our product quality system, and set stringent requirements for product reliability.

Among more than 50 suppliers, we stood out as the sole supplier awarded the business, and we solidified our reputation for product reliability and outstanding local service.

Thinking Like Top Customers

I liked to sit facing the big windows in the Sunrun's spacious conference room on the 29th floor that overlooks the landscape of San Francisco. I enjoyed having many meetings there with a wide range of stakeholders, most of whom were talented engineers. They gave us various customer requirements, we presented our product improvements, or we jointly explored creative solutions.

Many entrepreneurs have certain assumptions about products that may not necessarily hold true.

Some believe that the more advanced a product's technical features, the better it will fare in the market.

Some think that investing more money in product development will increase their chances of success.

However, blindly following these assumptions can result in high product development costs, without necessarily delighting customers or driving great business sales.

I challenged these assumptions, having learned from my big effort of leading our solar inverter local product development, testing, standard compliance and certifications, and technical trainings in the United States.

We were a small bird among industry giants. We couldn't afford the same level of high product development investments as the competition could. Not having all the flavors often found in our world-class competitors' products, our products were more like the plain vanilla ice cream.

Despite these limitations, we won over top customers, nationally and globally.

Our solar inverters gained a reputation for being reliable.

The key lesson here is not to let the assumptions of the cost and effort of product development hold you back from working with top customers.

I want to unveil a unique product strategy in the minds of top customers, in the Zen spirit, covering:
1) Design for Service
2) Design for Supply Chain
3) Design for Marketing

Products are at the heart of every business, but it's important to approach them, beyond products.

You may save hundreds of thousands of dollars on product development while growing profitable sales.

Product Design for Service

Thousands of our white, elegant solar inverters were shipped nationwide for local installations, and an engineering letter went out with each one of them.

I worked with our national electrical code expert to carefully craft this letter, certifying the products' compliance with the electrical code of each local jurisdiction, of which there are thousands in the nation.

In this letter, we also explained the unique design of our solar rapid shutdown device, for ease of installation with the popular solar racking systems, along with our inverters, to hundreds of solar installers nationwide.

When designing a product, it is crucial to consider how it can help reduce service cost, allowing for easier, faster, and cheaper service delivery.

Designing Products for Service may result in substantial cost savings while simultaneously delighting customers in the life cycle of product deployment.

First, product design should address the potential installation and implementation efforts.

For instance, we redesigned the solar inverter mounting plates to be installed on various wall surfaces nationwide. Our re-designed rapid shutdown devices also saved our client on installation labor cost.

Second, product design should address the potential maintenance effort.

For instance, we designed the monitoring devices to detect product issues remotely as early as possible to reduce expensive service trips and prevent future product issues. We conducted in-depth data-driven fault analyses for each issue.

Third, product design should address the potential service returns.

For instance, we designed product barcode tracking, built into our CRM-driven service support infrastructure, which allowed for customer self-service product return trackings and not only delighted customers but also saved us a great deal on our service costs.

Product Design for Supply Chain

I received a picture of a damaged pallet of our inverters from Sunrun's service department. This pallet had travelled over continents, spending days on the ocean, trains, and trucks, and had suffered from harsh transportation handling. We could not offer any excuses. We replaced these inverters for our top customers, and brought them back over the ocean, and on trains and trucks for repair at the factory where they were born. It was a very costly service, taking quite a few weeks.

Designing products with the supply chain in mind can result in substantial cost savings while simultaneously making customers happy.

First, it is crucial to consider how product design can help reduce shipping costs.

We designed smaller and lighter products that can be safely stacked in shipping containers to minimize shipping costs, a significant portion of the product landed cost.

International shipments, often managed by large logistics companies, charge high shipping fees. We want to consider factors such as product packaging shape, size, and weight during product design.

Second, product design should address the potential quality issues during the rigors of shipping.

Products that travel long distances through various transportation modes are susceptible to damage and quality problems. It is far more cost-effective to address and resolve these product issues at the factory rather than upon arrival at customer locations. By prioritizing quality control management, sturdy packaging, and protective measures, we can ensure that our products reach customers in optimal condition.

Third, product design should consider the ease of distribution for customers.

Shipping products to various locations can be a costly endeavor. To mitigate this, we can design products with customer distribution such as cross-docking in mind. For example, by analyzing customer domestic shipping patterns, we determined the optimal pallet size to allow for direct unloading from the ocean shipping containers and facilitate easy shipment to customer locations nationwide. This value-added service reduces customer shipping costs and enhances their overall experience with us.

Product Design for Marketing

"Why did you change your inverter packaging color from premium white to low-grade brown?"

I was lost and surprised when I received this uncomfortable phone call from a top customer's strategic sourcing director, whose voice was normally warm. In fact, I didn't know about this product change. It didn't follow the standard product change process in place with our top customer.

This decision was made solely by the headquarters' marketing team. They explained the reason—the change of packaging color was to save on material costs.

However, what they failed to recognize was the significant impact this color change would have on our brand reputation, which took years, huge effort from many people, and some good luck to build. The brown product packaging downgraded our premium brand image, leaving our top customers with a sense of confusion and disappointment.

Our client promptly rejected the color change, forcing the packaging to be changed back to the original premium white.

The small cost-saving benefits of a packaging design decision cannot come at the expense of compromising the brand's integrity.

This experience taught us a valuable lesson—the product design choices made for marketing must align with the brand aura we aim to illuminate. Product designing for marketing is a critical aspect that should never be overlooked, as it directly impacts the brand reputation.

Every element of visual aesthetic, including the color of the packaging, must be carefully considered to evoke the peak emotions in the minds of our top customers.

Standards, Not Stacks of Papers

Picture me sitting in the Moon Creek Sunroom, gazing at the serene woods, while my thoughts fly thousands of miles away to the islands of the Pacific Ocean. I pondered how we could accelerate solar adoption on these twenty-two islands to fight climate change.

The challenges I faced in Barbados in the past served as a valuable lesson. We had developed solar inverters compliant with the local utility standards, only to encounter a sudden change in their grid requirements. This shift rendered our products incompatible, losing sales opportunities, after spending months on the product development effort.

Determined not to repeat the Barbados experience in the Pacific Islands, I proposed a ground-breaking solution when providing my consulting advice to a renowned solar social impact company in Hawaii. We would not tackle each island's solar standards individually. By collectively standardizing the utility grid solar standards requirements across all twenty-two Pacific islands at the onset of the solarization efforts, we could significantly reduce implementation time from several years to less than a year. Millions of dollars would be saved by local utilities, solar equipment manufacturers, solar service companies, etc.

Standards are not merely a stack of documents collecting dust on shelves.

In fact, they serve as our gateway to accessing top customers in our niche market.

However, many entrepreneurs shy away from the challenges associated with achieving and implementing product standards, often relegating them to a low priority. It's time to change this perception and understand the true values that standards bring to your business.

In the state of California, as part of their grid modernization initiatives, concerns arose regarding solar saturation and the stability of the power grid, preventing the big solar adoptions. To address these issues, we would comply with the new solar data communication standards, hard requirements, and ensure that our smart inverters could intelligently communicate with the grids. This would enable them to respond to grid disturbances and prevent mass blackouts or brownouts. I asked our product team to contribute to the standard formation, while I joined the board of SunSpec Alliance, a leading international solar data communication standard non-profit organization.

Although it required several months of dedicated effort, we successfully achieved solar inverter compliance with these standards, allowing us to retain our top customers. As a result, we found ourselves competing with only a handful of companies in the solar inverter market, and we were perfectly positioned to become an industry leader.

It's now your turn to set your business apart from the competition. Seek out professional standard organizations in your niche market, join their ranks, and actively contribute to the industry development effort.

Products Tests via Third-Party

Visualize a white inverter, standing gracefully above the ocean waves, having withstood the fury of typhoons. Solar inverters often find homes in harsh environments, whether it's scorching heat, freezing cold, salty air, or arid dryness, all across the globe.

During the Solar Power International, a delighted young businessman approached me, praising the reliability of our inverters. While such compliments were music to my ears, I knew that words alone would not convince top banks and our top customers to invest in our products.

To win top customers, we partnered with a leading third-party solar equipment testing lab in Oakland, California to conduct rigorous reliability testing. By simulating challenging environments within the controlled settings of the testing lab, we could evaluate the equipment's performance under extreme conditions. Successfully passing these stringent tests would enable reliable operation of our solar inverters in diverse environmental conditions, over the lifetime of the equipment, across the globe. Some manufacturers chose to forgo the challenges of rigorous product reliability testing. Many of them disappeared from the market over the years. We pressed forward with determination, committed to delivering the highest quality to our customers.

Product design is not just about incorporating advanced technologies; product reliability plays a significant role in product differentiation.

Testing products rigorously before launching them in the market is crucial for avoiding future headaches, dramatically reducing service costs, and safeguarding long-term brand reputation.

We became the first inverter brand globally to pass the

rigorous third-party solar inverter reliability testing. We joined the Approved Vendor Lists of top banks and leading solar companies.

More importantly, we significantly enhanced product reliability by incorporating the findings from these rigorous tests into our R&D efforts and quality management systems.

It is advantageous that solar equipment unable to pass such rigorous reliability tests is not installed universally. The service costs associated with field failures can skyrocket, reaching as high as $300 to $400 per service trip in a labor-intensive market like the United States. A manufacturer with high field failure rates would struggle to survive under these conditions.

Product Quality, Invisible to the Eye

"What our eyes cannot see, our hearts can feel."

– Susanna Huang

"I found a quality issue!" exclaimed the serious-faced German engineer, his voice tinged with excitement. We all gathered around, and I peered through the magnifying glass. But I couldn't see anything, which puzzled me.

Our largest client, Sunrun, had arranged for six senior inverter engineers from three countries—Germany, the United States, and China—to conduct a factory inspection. I was leading them in an on-site inspection of the production line and product quality system at the factory.

The German engineer had previously served as the head of product development for a top European inverter brand. Holding a magnifying glass in one hand and an integrated circuit board in the other, he pointed to a component solder joint on the board, smaller than a mung bean.

The solder joint had a dent, not meeting the process standard of being completely filled, and the finished product inspection at the factory did not detect it at the time. If the inverter was in a vibrating state, such as during rough transportation, the component could detach from the circuit board, leading to product failure. Considering that the product would be installed in various natural environmental conditions across the globe, particularly in the labor-intensive United States, the consequences of quality issues were very serious.

Shortly afterward, the factory purchased more advanced soldering and quality testing machines. We didn't think the German Engineer was fussing over something insignificant but felt grateful for his keen eye. We appreciated his insight for early detection of the product's reliability issues in the barely visible details.

Product reliability starts with the entrepreneurs' intentions, and then flows into corporate cultures.

Before winning top-tier clients, are you willing to invest in the product quality first? The priority of product reliability tests the entrepreneur's mindset and determination.

Product Roadmaps for the Future

"Listen more, talk less."

– Susanna Huang

I was in a North America Headquarters building in Silicon Valley with a group of business professionals from Flex, a global Fortune 500 manufacturer. This was the same group of people I had worked with about one year before at SunEdison, once the world's largest renewable energy development company before its bankruptcy. Flex bought a portion of SunEdison's solar business.

We discussed our solar inverter product roadmaps. I said little in the meeting, while the VP of Global Product and his colleagues happily shared their beautiful product visions. They were top solar experts. I would do better just listening. Over the next few months, I worked with several Flex product engineers in different countries to gather their product requirements. Our product development accelerated, and the Flex team was happy to see our product development progress according to their product roadmaps.

One often overlooked but highly effective product strategy is to define a product roadmap that aligns with the needs foreseen by top customers. While many businesses rely on market research and competitor analysis for product development, these traditional sources can sometimes lead to high marketing research costs and offer little insight when the market landscape is in big shifts.

A well-crafted product roadmap typically spans one to three years, and serves as a guiding light for internal product development initiatives. Top customers possess invaluable insights into market trends and future product requirements, so they can provide more precise guidance for our product development efforts. This alignment allows us to allocate our resources strategically, minimizing our product development costs while maximizing our chances of success. Our top customers are also delighted.

Service is Sales, in Enso Circles

"Service is Not Second Sales. Service is Sales."

– Susanna Huang

Once the global market leader, our German Solar Inverter competitor had around 20 service people in California, we had only two service engineers nationwide.

Sunrun, our top customer, required us to have world-class service to do business with us.

A new brand with little established local service and experience, we were benchmarked against world-class competitors known for world-class service. And we were at risk of losing our contract with Sunrun if we did not comply. We were facing huge business risks.

However, as someone who was well-trained at Accenture, I saw the opportunities to rise in service.

The advances in IT technologies had carried traditional services into the modern age, with only a fraction of the traditional development and operation cost.

I architected, designed, and worked with our team of engineers to build our world-class service support infrastructure ahead of the curve, even before we had secured big orders. As a result, our service was able to scale quickly and reliably with the sudden ramp-up of solar installations nationwide, from a few hundred to more than twenty thousand installations annually. What's more, while having only less than one tenth of the service workforce, we were still able to provide a high-standard service, quantified in Service Level Agreement KPI Key Performance Indicator measurements, delighting our top customers.

In my experience, the common assumptions that service is not as important as sales, and that building an efficient service support infrastructure is too costly, are simply not true, and often lead us astray.

In fact, service was one of the main reasons our company was able to win the prestigious Top PV Brand award from EuPD, a leading market and opinion research institute, who surveyed the opinions of the installers nationwide.

I discovered, Service is Sales, and a solid service support infrastructure is the key to success.

Service is Sales, Not Second Sales

At a solar trade show, the US general manager of our German Solar Inverter competitor talked to me about his belief that "Service is second Sales." I nodded in agreement, while quietly erasing "second" in my mind. He built a world-class service in the United States, respected by many people in the industry.

But I believe that "Service is Sales".

When I rode in the heavy-duty truck with a young service technician, driving around the city to perform the annual calibration of the truck scales, my colleague would regularly chat happily with the customer manager. I saw first-hand how excellent service can benefit a company in the long run.

Working at Mettler Toledo, a Fortune 500 global manufacturer in its North America Headquarter in Columbus, Ohio, confirmed to me that service is a crucial part of a well-respected business.

Many people may see service as just blue-collar work, but it is so much more than that.

"Service is Sales" is a paradigm shift that can help businesses gain a new vision for their service program.

By viewing service as a vital aspect of sales, companies can develop a best-in-class service program that brings in more sales and creates greater brand reputation, which is both cost-effective to build and run, difficult for competitors to replicate, and a key market differentiator.

Join me on this journey to develop a new service strategy.

Business Selling Service

I suggested our salespeople not only to carry our product brochures, but also carry the value propositions of our unique service program when visiting clients.

Great service is a part of our overall solution that we sell to customers.

In my experience, many customers choose to walk away from a manufacturer with great technologies but a weak local service program. This highlights the importance of a strong local service program, one of the three keywords in our brand propositions I created: Bankable. Reliable. Local Service.

While we can see, feel, and touch a product, we cannot experience the service before it's delivered. Yet, our reliable service is crucial to our customer's success. Customers often predict our service quality based on our service track records, with such data coming from KPI data in our service support infrastructure.

In the highly competitive market, a business brand needs to stand out and be unique. However, with the product development cycle accelerating, it's getting harder to differentiate products in the crowd. On the other hand, a best-in-class service program that is intricately designed, implemented, and fine-tuned over time is unique, and much more difficult for competitors to imitate.

Selling service is not just about gaining the trust of our customers, it's also about providing a unique competitive advantage that sets us apart from others.

Service Keeping Sales

Once the sales transactions were completed, our service team took over most customer interactions.

In the minds of our top customers, our service also became their service. If we didn't deliver service timely or failed to meet their expectations, their customers would not be happy either. Our services were measured in their services to customers. The cost of losing customer satisfaction is probably much higher than the product's value itself—potentially losing the trust or even sales of their customers.

As entrepreneurs, we all know that the cost of keeping an existing customer is likely much lower than that of acquiring a new one. A great service program helps businesses keep their sales cost-effectively.

Our solar product is expected to last over 20 years, just like the truck scales I used to work on. If our service falls apart, we risk losing our hard-earned customers forever. That's why we made a conscious decision to invest in a comprehensive, easy to scale service program ahead of the curve.

We provided best-in-class service across multiple contact points with multiple stakeholders of our top customers, such as the design crew, training professionals, and field installers. We have built close, resilient relationships that are hard to break by other competitors.

A great service program takes time to build and mature. It's not a quick fix, but it's an investment that pays off in the long run. With a well-designed and implemented service program, we can keep our customers happy, and that means keeping our sales, with little cost.

Sales Coming from Service

Our service people interact with customers more frequently than the salespeople in our customer business relationships. They have greater opportunities to influence customer perceptions of our business.

Service people who provide excellent service not only strengthen customer relationships but also have opportunities to promote our products or services with ease with customers.

Sales are a possible by-product of excellent service. We are known for services with outstanding BBB A+ ratings. Customers tend to trust the advice of service professionals more than that of salespeople. This trust factor often leads to repeat business and recommending our business to others.

It is crucial to invest in the personal development and brand education of service people, who not only attend to current sales but may also create new sales opportunities.

Service Trends

We implemented a best-in-class service strategy with low cost. Achieving these two goals together might seem challenging, but it is possible if you follow the major trends in service.

Self-Service

Our service portal has garnered over one million views; some were from overseas.

People come to find our field-proven answers to their solar inverter or installation questions on their own.

Self-service is a game-changer. It simply means that we don't do it. Instead, we let the customers do it.

Customers have more control and freedom to get the service they need from our business, when and where they need it, and in the way they want.

This approach satisfies customers' preferences and results in significantly lower service costs for us, their supplier and service provider—a truly creative win-win solution.

Artificial Intelligence for Service

A cute little Chatbot blinks on the corner of our service portal screen. It's incredible how Artificial Intelligence (AI) has become a readily available CRM built-in tool, Chatbot, that empowers users to get the service they need when they need it.

With AI, we can achieve self-service with human-like quality. AI-powered chatbots and virtual assistants have revolutionized customer service. They can handle multiple customer interactions simultaneously, and they learn from each interaction to improve their responses. AI has made self-service efficient and effective, enabling businesses to provide 24/7 support at a lower cost.

With AI, we can create a service experience that is seamless, personalized, and responsive.

Service Automation

Every service process of our business was designed, streamlined, documented, and implemented into our knowledge base. In the meanwhile, these service processes are also built into our customized CRM platform with automation functions. Service reports are also generated automatically to measure the service performance.

Service automation is a crucial element of a best-in-class service strategy.

By standardizing and optimizing business processes over years, we dramatically improved our service reliability and delivery speed, while also reducing our labor costs.

From AI-powered chatbots to cloud-based CRM solutions, automation can help service providers stay ahead of the competition and deliver exceptional, reliable service, achieving high productivity and efficiency.

Customized Service Solutions

We provide an individual service portal catering to each customer's needs. With advanced CRM technologies, we can also offer bespoke services to small customers.

This personalized approach ensures our customers receive

the highest level of service and support, which is highly important to them, and helps us build trust and loyalty with them over time.

Our customized service solutions help us deliver world-class service.

Customized Service Solutions are key to building strong and lasting customer relationships. Each customer is unique, which is why they enjoy tailored service solutions to meet their specific requirements.

Take the time to listen to customers, understand their goals and objectives, and then design a customized service program to delight them.

"SOAK" in Service, Best-in-Class

Now let's look at "SOAK" in Service, a unique service strategy to build a best-in-class service program with low cost.
S – Self-Service.
O – Outsource.
A – Automation.
K – Knowledge base.

S – Self-Service.

I used to run large strategic sourcing projects for Fortune 500 Companies in IT areas, and I have observed self-service being offered in this industry.

What if our customers could self-service? I pondered. They would have much more freedom. It could also greatly reduce our effort to serve them, and we would spend less money on service, while still keeping customers happy.

For instance, let's take the example of our solar inverter service ticketing system.

On the user-friendly interface of our service portal, Installers can log a ticket to report a solar inverter issue, find potential solutions in our knowledge base, or chat with our AI-powered associate. They can check their issue ticket status until it is resolved, and receive an automatically generated customized report periodically.

It's a win-win situation for both customers and businesses.

O – Outsource.

The demand for our service fluctuates constantly, and we could not afford to have our service people sitting idle during low-demand periods. At the same time, we could not sacrifice customer experience by failing to train new hires for service tasks on time. I decided to outsource the overflow of our services, keeping only major services in house.

By outsourcing to a third-party call center, tasks are allocated dynamically among their trained associates across their multiple customer accounts. This effort kept our overall operation costs low and allowed us to adjust call center usage according to demand, thus lowering the cost while maintaining high service levels.

Outsourcing is a common practice across many industries, and it can help businesses save money on service.

However, it's important to choose trustworthy partners. We must be cautious when selecting outsourcing partners to ensure they are aligned with our values, trustworthy, and reliable, preventing any potential risks and losses to our business.

A – Automation

After driving by the Salesforce building in San Francisco, out of curiosity, I decided to study their modern industry leading CRM (Customer Relationship Management) solutions thoroughly.

I quickly realized that without CRM, we would struggle to meet the stringent service-level requirements of our top customers, modelled after our world-class competitors. This was especially so when our service demand ramped up dramatically, from several hundred to tens of thousands of installations nationwide within a year.

Automation is a key factor in improving operation efficiencies and lowering service costs. We harness the power of cutting-edge cloud-based CRM solutions to automate our service operations.

At Accenture Consulting, I learned that the best people for CRM implementations were not in IT, but business professionals. I architected, designed, and implemented our customized CRM solutions with ultra-simplicity, and assigned our experienced service engineers to work on detailed processed design and implementations.

We simplified and standardized our service processes based on industry best practices, before building them into our CRM platform to save implementation effort.

All customer interactions, including emails, calls, online inquiries, and social media interactions, regardless of the size of the customer, are processed and tracked end-to-end in transactions with speed, consistency, and reliability. Our customers are delighted with the quality of service they receive.

K – Knowledge base

Our service team possesses a wealth of knowledge on solar inverter technologies, with years of solar industry experience.

I designed a knowledge base infrastructure to help our team to "download" knowledge from their minds into an easily accessible database, covering a wide range of topics, akin to a library with books lined up on shelves.

Initially, the knowledge base was only intended for internal use. But I later saw the value of sharing knowledge and decided to make certain content available to the public through our service portal.

Let's take a closer look at the profound impact of our knowledge base.

One of our PV inverter technical articles has been viewed nearly 15,000 times. If we assume that it takes one minute to read, we can estimate the cost savings for our service engineers as follows.

With an annual labor cost of approximately US$80k per engineer, the availability of this one article alone saves about US$10,000 in our internal service labor costs. And that's just one article! With hundreds of articles in our knowledge base, which I asked our engineers to create over the years, the total internal service cost savings add up significantly.

The sharing of industry-specific knowledge is essential for providing efficient service and enabling customers to help themselves through self-service.

The results were remarkable, even unbelievable.

Our service portal attracted over a million views globally with its high-quality contents and ease of use interfaces, and it soon became an unexpected brand marketing tool. It not only greatly improved our brand awareness, but also required little third-party marketing expenses.

Keeping the knowledge base fresh and relevant also helped attract new customers.

Our knowledge base is a powerful tool that supports our unique low-cost, high-performance service strategy.

Service Smarter in "ABC"

Service is evolving and becoming smarter and more intelligent in three key areas:

A - Artificial Intelligence (AI)

AI revolutionized service operations. It enables high service levels while reducing operational costs.

B - Business Intelligence

We can make smarter data-driven business decisions using data captured in our service platform.

We can design Key Performance Indicators (KPIs) tailored to the specific requirements of our customers, enabling us to improve service quality and customer satisfaction while identifying areas of opportunity for service improvements and cost savings.

We can benchmark against the best practices of our industry and across industries, becoming a market leader.

C - Circle of Intelligence

Service is where the rubber meets the road. It is where we interact with customers for the longest period of time, making it a valuable source of feedback about our products.

We want to pass on the insights obtained from service throughout the life cycle of sustainable design, manufacturing, and supply chain, even to the landfill, to continuously improve our products and delight our customers.

With a circle of intelligence from service, we grow better every day.

Training as Service, Unexpected

We provided monthly technical training workshops nationwide, mostly with industry-leading experts, accompanied by our own engineer speakers. Each online workshop attracted one hundred to three hundred people, similar to the size of industry-leading marketing workshops.

Training can be an unexpected yet impactful service offering for businesses, yielding three main benefits.

Marketing Alternative

For startups and businesses with limited marketing budgets, training-as-service can be an effective supplemental marketing tool. It offers a cost-effective alternative to traditional marketing efforts and can be easily implemented under the procurement authority of business leaders, without the need for lengthy approvals of marketing budgets, reaching a wider audience faster, and more cost effectively.

Sales Lead Generation

Training participants can be warm leads with high potential for sales conversions. By following up with each participant, internal sales can qualify sales leads, leaving more costly experienced salespeople to focus on high-potential warm leads, yielding higher sales conversion rates with low investment.

Customer Training

Continuous technical training can build long-term trust with customers. Professional training provided within the company's exclusive community strengthens the customer relationship. And long-term trust may translate into sales results at the right time.

Sell Values with Courage

> "Selling is to exchange values through interconnectedness."
>
> – Susanna Huang

I hired some experienced, high-paid salespeople, expecting them to generate high sales. Our sales tanked.

These old-fashioned salespeople didn't believe we could sell to big customers. Our US business was much smaller with less brand recognition compared to their former, much bigger employers. So, they could not sell to big customers, instead, they stayed in their comfort zones with small sales.

In contrast, I was a new salesperson. Sometimes our courage comes from being new, not knowing it is not possible to sell our products to big customers. My strategies of selling to big customers, with experience gained from leading the strategic sourcing consulting projects for Fortune 500 companies, turned out to be fruitful and cost-effective in the long run.

While the initial cost of selling was high, big sales costs are much lower compared to the sum of the cost of selling to small customers repeatedly. Many of our competitors disappeared from the market, chasing only small customers, and then losing them one by one.

There are two common assumptions about sales that some people believe to be true, that turn out to be false:

Experienced, high-paid salespeople can bring in more sales revenues. And selling to big customers costs significantly more than selling to smaller ones.

Business Partnership vs. Transactions

When the ink in my pen runs out, I buy a new box of pens from an online distributor on Amazon—this represents a transactional relationship. Transactional relationships are fragile; customers can easily switch suppliers.

With our big customers, we built business partnerships—an interdependent relationship. While many companies tend to engage in simple transactions, developing a true business partnership holds greater value, and should be carefully considered.

Solar equipment has a lifespan of over twenty years. When major clients choose solar equipment, they are also selecting to engage in a long-term business collaboration with the equipment manufacturer. We interact with the different functional areas of our clients, from research and development to design, manufacturing, testing, delivery, installation, after-sales, and disposal throughout the entire product lifecycle. If, for any reason, our inverters fail to arrive on time and cannot meet the scheduled installation time for the major clients and their customers, it would negatively impact our customers' business reputation.

Even though our business was small at the beginning, we had the courage to become a business partner with industry-leading big clients.

There were numerous benefits:

First, the orders from our top customers resolved our urgent need for funds. Major clients, often concerned about their industry reputation, are more likely to make timely payments, which reduces the likelihood of delaying our payments.

Second, top customers are typically willing to provide technical expertise to guide our localized research and development effort, thus enabling us to advance localized technology with minimal investment.

Third, the brand effect of major top customers makes it easier for us to gain the trust and get orders from other high-quality top customers.

I will explain how to manage the intricate sales process to top customers, which I did not learn from other sales in the solar industry.

Thinking Like Big Customers

For years, I led large complex strategic sourcing projects for Fortune 500 companies, which gave me the opportunity to observe the customer sales experience from the other side of the negotiation table. With this understanding, I was able to win big, world-class customers in the solar industry.

Understanding the perspective of big customers can be the key to unlocking success.

It requires a paradigm shift in how we approach big sales, but with the right strategy, selling to big customers can be cost-effective and profitable.

First, we sell our company credentials.

We share our heart-touching business stories that shaped our business in critical moments to build a foundation of trust in our business relationship, positioning us as a reliable business partner.

We present our current business performance to showcase our capabilities for collaboration.

We paint a vivid vision of our business's future, instilling confidence as a committed long-term partner.

Second, we sell our products.

It's critical to understand the unique product requirements of top customers by tapping into multiple sources, including their current product usage, and requesting information or proposal documents.

We highlight key product features that align seamlessly with their needs, for example, emphasizing proven product reliability over advanced technologies in our solar inverter sales.

Then we outline our product roadmaps. Even though there may be short-term gaps with their needs, we showcase our commitment to tailored solutions and mutual growth.

Third, we concentrate on the power of selling our service.

It is essential to recognize the pivotal role of service in their decision-making process.

We immerse ourselves in their service requirements, exploring requests for information and proposal documents, and analyzing the service provided by existing suppliers.

We then showcase our historical service Key Performance Indicator (KPI) data, accompanied by glowing testimonials from satisfied users.

However, what truly inspires confidence is a well-established service support infrastructure that ensures the quality delivery of service consistently over time.

Fourth, confidence is paramount when selling pricing.

Our product pricing is not the lowest, but it's not the highest either. Challenge the misconception that lower pricing guarantees success in sales.

Big customers value the reasonable profit margins of their suppliers when seeking long-term business partnerships. Some may request access to our cost books for pricing transparency.

Present a fair and reasonable pricing model tied to sales volumes or industry indices.

Focus on the value proposition your products and services bring, solidifying your dedication to a mutually beneficial, long-term partnership.

Fifth, we delve into the world of value-added services.

Often overlooked, the value-added services can revolutionize your relationship with top customers.

We envision our organization and the top customer as one cohesive entity, seeking overlapping functions that can be optimized or eliminated. By leveraging our unique capabilities, we lower costs and forge stronger bonds with top customers, leading to increased profitability.

Educate them on the possibilities of adding values they

may not even be aware of.

Harness the power of company credentials, product excellence, exceptional service, fair pricing, and value-added services. By thinking like top customers, we become an invaluable business partner with top customers in our pursuit of greatness together for the long term.

Many-to-Many Collaborations

The new director at Sunrun said to me, "You know more people in our company than I do." That was true.

I had a customer stakeholder matrix. It illustrated the roles and responsibilities of each key player I worked with over the years within the big organization. I gained invaluable insights into the intricate dynamics at play using this visual representation, and by engaging in meaningful conversations, delving deep into each key stakeholder's unique requirements, aspirations, and pain points.

Our focus extends beyond short-term sales, and more on building enduring business partnerships.

Selling to top customers is not a mere one-to-one interaction; It requires a well-crafted strategy, taking a many-to-many approach to engage various stakeholders.

Our aim is to comprehend the big picture of our customers' business strategies and align our business to support their goals, like we are part of them. By doing so, we forge resilient, long-term partnerships and propel mutual success.

Some stakeholders have the potential to become our internal champions, guiding us through the vast corridors of the big corporation, connecting us with invaluable resources, or even advocating for our offerings within our top customer's organization. It is important to dedicate time and effort to nurturing these precious and valuable personal business relationships.

Moreover, we assembled a multi-functional team within our organization to support the big sales effort. Together, we bring in diverse perspectives and knowledge and harness the collective wisdom of our team to navigate the complex landscape of top customers. This ensures a comprehensive understanding of the multifaceted needs of the top customer and helps us deliver solutions accordingly.

When we redesigned our cutting-edge solar inverters for ease of mounting with the solar racking system and achieved local code compliance nationwide, we took a collaborative approach with our top customers. This yielded remarkable results, generating significant cost savings due to streamlined installations and inspections for thousands of solar installation projects nationwide.

By combining our expertise with that of our top customers, we unlock a world of possibilities and deliver exceptional value. The collective knowledge and resources of each collaborator enhance the overall solution, ensuring that every aspect of the product meets the highest standards of quality, functionality, and compliance.

Collaborative selling solidified our position as industry leaders.

A Fresh Sales Perspective

In the enchanting realm of sales, sometimes a shift in perspective is all it takes to unlock new possibilities. Think beyond sales, consider the factors that impact sales, think about interconnectedness.

Allow these five transformative questions to guide you on your journey:

#1: Is your investment in marketing sufficient to fuel your sales efforts?

Picture a delicate dance between investing wisely in marketing and reaping the rewards of increased sales. Are you allocating enough resources at the right time on marketing, or are you holding back, fearing the uncertain returns?

#2: Do you have an ample sales force to conquer nationwide territories?

Imagine a tapestry of nationwide opportunities waiting to be seized. Do you find yourself limited by a tight budget that restricts your ability to hire sufficient salespeople? Are there any collaborative opportunities to leverage other business partners' sales forces?

#3: Are you harnessing the potential of your internal sales team?

Peer behind the curtain of your organization and uncover the untapped potential within your internal sales team. Are they solely occupied with traditional back-office work, or can they be empowered to generate warm sales leads for experienced, higher-paid salespeople?

#4: Are you accessing a bountiful pool of high-quality sales leads?

Imagine a wellspring of sales leads, abundant and of exceptional quality. Are you patiently relying on organic growth, or can you seek out additional avenues to expand your pipeline?

#5: Can you forge lasting, trustworthy customer relationships, even from a distance?

Visualize a world where building meaningful customer relationships transcends physical boundaries. With travel restrictions and higher costs, traditional sales visits may be limited. Explore innovative ways to cultivate trust and rapport remotely, unlocking the potential for long-term partnerships.

As you ponder these transformative questions, let them guide you towards new perspectives on sales.

A problem well-stated is indeed half-solved.

Marketing is Attraction

"Marketing is Attraction, Resonating in Hearts, not Just Appealing in Eyes."

– Susanna Huang

I decided to release our series of short service videos, the ones being laughed at due to "poor quality," on our 24/7 service portal, and also encouraged our people to distribute them to help solar installers nationwide.

We had little local marketing and training budget, but our service calls were increasing quickly with our fast-growing number of solar equipment shipments, which were thousands nationwide. I still liked my creative idea of asking our product engineers to produce these service videos in their spare time during work, as we promote them ourselves and don't pay for third-party marketing.

Our short service videos worked beyond our expectations, garnering several hundreds of thousands of views over three years, far more views than the professionally made expensive videos.

Marketing is often misunderstood.

Many believe that marketing is solely the responsibility of the marketing department.

Some believe that spending more money on glamorous marketing guarantees better sales results.

While there is some truth to these assumptions, they can lead to costly expenditures, especially in the marketing, often referred to as an expensive cost center.

But there is much more to marketing. Marketing is Attraction.

Marketing is about capturing the hearts and souls of people and drawing them to our products and services, following the law of attraction, through various channels.

Traditional marketing certainly has its place in business, but there are newer, more effective options to explore.

In the early stages of my business, I wrote articles for top magazines in the United States and India, leveraging the power of free personal brand marketing.

As our business grew, we invested hundreds of dollars in advertisements, only to see minimal results.

It was when our engineers who performed the marketing initiatives that our service portal became one of the most important marketing channels. It garnered over one million views.

Marketing goes beyond these superficial elements.

Marketing Aligned with Brand

I carefully crafted our solar inverter market advertising slogan. They are simple, only three, Zen-inspired words:
1) Bankable. What others lacked, we possessed, backed by top-tier banks.
2) Reliable. Where others were adequate, we excelled, being the first solar inverter brand globally to pass the most stringent third-party product reliability tests.
3) Local. Where others were competent, we stood out, with products and an efficient and bespoke service system.

Each word represents the accumulation and refinement of our business efforts over the years.

In an era when people were concerned about the quality issues prevalent in the solar inverter market, each word gave customers peace of mind.

What customers perceive and are moved by, is not what we strive to present to them, but our "true self." Some marketing programs try to create a brand image to attract customers, it is not effective. People are attracted by who we are.

As an unknown solar inverter brand in the early days, using these techniques, we left a mark in our customers' minds without investing in extravagant advertising, and achieved a top global brand.

Let's set aside traditional marketing methods and delve into the effective and intriguing marketing strategies that we have verified in practice.

Rooted in Brand Essence

I shared the importance of discovering and nurturing the deep roots of our brand essence, the soul seed of the founder. However, in the real world, I have observed that companies invest their resources in areas that are disconnected from the essence of their brands.

It's common to see advertisements highlighting product features like those of their competitors, neglecting the core value propositions of the brand. Those expensive, movie-like ads with high video production costs fail to capture the audience's hearts.

Brand encompasses everything we do, including marketing, and should reflect the interconnections of different functional areas of the business.

Marketing is not just the job of marketing departments. In our case, our service engineers also did a great job on marketing.

Could you look beyond your marketing department to conduct marketing?

Peak Emotions Captured

During a solar trade show, I had the opportunity to meet a solar veteran who had installed our inverter at his ranch over a decade before. He spoke to me with great excitement, sharing that our inverter had been running reliably for all those years. His words touched me deeply, as it was the emotions behind them that truly resonated.

To truly connect with your customers, it is essential to consciously observe, then capture the peak emotions that our products and services evoke in our customers. These peak emotions serve as the wellspring for marketing, endorsing the brand's messages in a way that parallels the impact of a heart-touching song.

Various Marketing Channels

It's crucial to connect with your audience through various channels.

People have their own preferences when it comes to accessing information. From websites and YouTube to TikTok, Facebook, Twitter, and WeChat, there are numerous social media communication channels available.

Through these channels, we presented the peak emotions captured in our products and services, in various formats, creating a cohesive experience within our system of social media, Enso's social media Solar System, my next topic.

Susanna Qiang Huang

Enso's Social Media Solar System

In the early days, I wrote articles for top solar magazines in the United States and India. However, as our business started to thrive, I found it increasingly challenging to dedicate enough time to writing, a task I enjoyed very much. So I put my social media passion on pause, assuming it would take too much time.

In today's business landscape, social media has emerged as the dominant marketing platform, presenting a tremendous opportunity for entrepreneurs. With a fraction of the traditional marketing budget, we can effectively reach a large audience, which is especially ideal for smaller business entrepreneurs.

People often form their initial impressions of a business through online surfing. In fact, they may already decide whether to trust a business enough to make a purchase before even meeting anyone in person from that business.

I put in a lot of effort searching for a magical social media strategy that would save hours and dollars.

One day, I discovered "Enso's Social Media Solar System."

Imagine our social media presence as a solar system, with the Sun at the center and the planets orbiting around it.

People choose their preferred channels to interact with us on various social media platforms, the planets, in their favorite format, such as text, video, or audio. Regardless of the social media platform they engage with, we bring them back to our Sun, which we define, for example, a website, a YouTube channel, etc.—it's up to you.

The effort we put into building Enso's Social Media Solar System upfront proved to be worthwhile, as eventually, the planets naturally gravitated toward the Sun.

By implementing this approach, we created a cohesive

and impactful social media presence that effectively engaged our audience and brought them closer to our brand, with lower financial investment and less time.

Contents Created with Ease

Let me share a secret to alleviate the stress of creating content for various social media platforms.

That is, creating a high-quality piece of content first and then repurposing it across multiple platforms.

For instance, a video can be transformed into a blog post or a podcast, saving valuable time and effort.

Videos

One day, my car wouldn't start. I panicked and quickly searched for "How to start a car" short videos on my iPhone. Following the instructions, I successfully started my car and felt an immense sense of pride.

This experience sparked an idea: our installers might appreciate short service videos too, as reading lengthy installation manuals was not enjoyable. I asked our engineers to produce service videos that have since garnered nearly 300,000 total views—without investing in any third-party marketing. We experienced improved installation quality, reduced service costs, and delightful customer relationships.

Our short 3-5 minute videos addressed customer problems individually, catering to short attention spans. What made these videos truly resonate with installers was our passion and authenticity. Our product engineers, who were also former installers, featured in these videos, creating a genuine emotional connection with the installers. The short videos were voluntarily shared by our engineers and installers to solve everyday installation problems. One such low-cost, imperfect video received 60K views.

Newsletters

Surprisingly, newsletters, an old tool, remain one of the most effective ways to connect with our audience. Our newsletters focus solely on news, sharing one update per letter, such as a new product release, a service offering, an upcoming trade show, or a training announcement. We diligently gather contacts from various sources, including trade shows, sales meetings, service interactions, and social media. By sending out newsletters personally and including a call to action, we create a sense of personal warmth that increases the likelihood of them being opened.

Blogs

To connect with the right people, I realized that I should not only share business-related topics but also my observations, insights, and personal stories. LinkedIn is my ideal platform, as it allows me to constantly engage with my classmates, co-workers, and professionals.

It is critical to have fresh information on LinkedIn business profiles, as they serve as our virtual business cards. The initial trust gained from LinkedIn connections can greatly accelerate future business collaborations.

Developing your own blogging style is essential. Personally, I prefer concise text accompanied by high-quality images, making it easy to produce while capturing the viewers' attention.

Find your own unique style that resonates with your audience.

Webinars

I asked our engineers to lead the technical training webinars instead of sales professionals. Speaking their language, our engineers established a strong rapport with the participants, who were mostly installers. There were genuine connections.

I invited solar experts to co-present, elevating our brand and expanding our circle of influence.

We conducted surveys before and after the webinars, asking simple questions to engage participants, and providing completion certificates as an incentive.

With the shift toward online meetings, a portion of in-person trainings has been replaced. However, I still cherish the warmth of client visits and the opportunity to explore new places, reminiscent of my consulting days at Accenture.

Different Brand Phases

A great brand touches the hearts of people, though different types of people, in various ways, at different phases in their lives. I've observed this phenomenon during the business growth in solar.

Drawing parallels between Apple and the solar inverter, I've noticed similar trajectories in their growth, which can be applied to any industry.

Germination Phase: Led by Dreams

During this phase, customers are often pioneers, driven by dreams and ideals, much like hobbyists and idealists.

Steve Jobs's involvement in "The Homebrew Computer Club" exemplifies this, as it was a space where enthusiasts passionately explored the future of computer technology in a nascent industry.

The solar industry had similar humble beginnings. One of our earliest customers, David, installed our inverters when solar equipment was quite expensive, more than 10 years ago. He melded his love for solar technology and his desire to live in harmony with nature, powering his ranch house, hiding in the California woods, with solar. David founded AEE Solar, one of the oldest and largest solar distributors, about 40 years ago, which was later acquired by SunRun, providing its distribution service.

Early Phase: Driven by Businesses

In the early days, customers mainly consisted of early adopters who were eager to embrace innovative technologies.

When Steve Jobs introduced the Apple II in April 1977, it marked a pivotal moment in the personal computer industry. Apple's performance, friendly design, and seamless user experience captivated these early adopters.

2015 was a lucky year for our solar business. I began to work with Sunrun and SolarCity—later acquired by Tesla—opening a unique opportunity to observe their businesses from the inside. Solar technologies were still quite expensive, but there were different kinds of incentives to lower the cost, which solar businesses actively promoted. The solar industry was growing but still quite small. Our marketing messages were filled with technical jargon that resonated with this tech-savvy audience.

At this stage, it became increasingly challenging to differentiate products solely on technologies.

Explosive Growth Phase: Loved by Consumers

During this stage, customers are drawn in by emotional connections.

Steve Jobs introduced the iPod in October 2001. Despite Sony's superior resources at the time, they couldn't replicate the success of the iPod. Jobs designed the iPod for music lovers, like himself. He understood their pain points and intuitively grasped the emotional experience and deep connection to music that the iPod provided. The marketing messages surrounding the iPod were deeply touching, such as the iconic tagline, "1000 songs in your pocket." The iPod bridged the gap between poetry and engineering, merging artistic creativity and technology, and resonated with millions of music lovers worldwide.

Consumers often seek products that bring them closer to their higher selves and evoke strong positive feelings.

For example, Apple electronics may evoke a feeling of world-changing geniuses. Tesla electric cars may evoke the feeling of a new human living in the future.

In 2021, the solar energy industry entered a new era of explosive growth, infiltrating the lives of millions of individuals in their homes and businesses. During this phase, we witnessed a shift in focus from technical jargon to the marketing messages that deeply touched people's hearts, like songs, like poetry.

Decline Phase: Recreating from Nothingness

Let's look at the story of Starbucks.

For years, people had grown accustomed to drinking mediocre coffee merely for a caffeine boost.

Mr. Schultz, the founder, took a trip to Italy and became fascinated with the unique coffee culture there. In the stagnant coffee industry, he established Starbucks, creating a brand-new industry from nothingness. Starbucks café became the "third place between home and work," spreading globally and captivating people all over the world. Drinking coffee was no longer an ordinary daily routine. Starbucks became one of the world's greatest business brands, miraculously "inspiring and nurturing the human spirit."

Every industry eventually comes to an end. Planning ahead allows us to capitalize on the last remaining profits. During the decline, customers gradually leave the brand. We often milk the cash cows of the declining brands.

However, I have also witnessed the most miraculous "creation from nothingness," where an exciting new industry emerged from what seemed to be a dying industry. For example, the fading iPod industry gave birth to the smartphone industry, much like a large tree falling, only to be replaced by the growth of new saplings.

Leaving or disrupting the old industry marks the beginning of a new industry, much like the waxing and waning of the moon.

Having been in an industry for a long time, we get accustomed to seeing, hearing, and thinking in a similar way as others. How can you create a unique and irreplicable competitive advantage for your business? For instance, when I went to repair my computer, I intentionally learned about the computer's after-sales service processes. Or when I selected health insurance for my employees, I learned about their self-service customer approaches.

Embark on a spontaneous journey of the mind and explore the magical world outside. There are many other business cases from various industries that can serve as inspiration. It's not about reading through thick industry analysis reports, half-asleep; it's about observing with keen attention, learning from other industries, and adapting and improving in our own industry.

Organizations are Like Water

"You put water into a bottle, it becomes the bottle. You put it in a teapot, it becomes the teapot. Water can flow, or it can crash. Be water, my friend."

– Bruce Lee

"Be Water, my business friend."

– Susanna Huang

"Susanna, thanks for sending over your business presentation. It looks nice."

"Susanna, what is the meaning of this error code?"

"Susanna, when will my order arrive at our warehouse?"

"Susanna, could you pay our bill this week?" ……

When I started my business, I did everything.

My headshot was in the box for each role in our organization chart.

I was bustling like a busy bee, a super busy working bee.

I had hoped all that would change after we won our first major top customer, Sunrun.

And I was able to hire more people. However, this was what happened:

"Susanna, please interview this engineer on Wednesday."

"Susanna, what do you want me to do?"

"Susanna, could you show me how to do it for the first time?"

"Susanna, could you review this document I put together before I submit it to the client?"

"Susanna, could you..."

Our business grew rapidly, which made me happy. On the other hand, my life didn't get any easier. More headshots replaced my headshot one by one in our organization chart, but employees frequently came to me seeking guidance. I was constantly stepping in to solve problems or resolve conflicts. Our organization's efficiency suffered. I was even busier, then got exhausted.

Decisions, that used to be made quickly and easily now required great coordination effort between different people across different business functions." The "water" in our business was either blocked or turned turbulent.

I wasn't alone in facing these challenges. I heard similar stories from other entrepreneurs.

So, how could we sail through turbulent waters with grace and speed?

Common beliefs in organization management are the following:
1) Clear-cut functional definitions make an organization more effective, and
2) Efficiency is gained from harmonizing business functions solely within an organization's boundaries.

However, I discovered a different organization strategy, upon which an award-winning business was built.

Intuitively, I applied the world-class project methodologies, which I learned during my happy days at Accenture and matured during my management consulting services to Fortune 500 companies.

Instead of following a traditional function-driven organization approach, I designed a new organization strategy for our young businesses, called PACKS.

P - Process Mapping
A - Accountability Assignment
C - Cross-Functional Team
K - KPI Measurement
S - Sharing Knowledge

Employing this strategy means a boutique business will not only appear big, but also perform like a big organization and win big.

"PACKS" Organization Strategy

P - Process Mapping

In the early days, I was a one-person show, wearing multiple hats to take charge of every aspect of business.

I made decisions quickly, moving like graceful water flows. My primary objectives were clear—drive sales, ensure efficient and cost-effective operations, and delight our customers.

However, as our business grew, I started to replace my headshot with others in our organizational chart.

The once graceful flows of our business processes were now broken, fragmented, and scattered. Unsurprisingly, our organizational efficiency declined. I was getting frustrated.

I began the process mapping, as I often did at Accenture, but taking a much simpler approach.

I "downloaded" those customer-centric, interconnected business processes from my head onto papers.

I documented each activity, assigned responsibilities, and analyzed interconnections between activities.

Process Mapping, the "P" in PACKS, revolves around customer-centric process mapping across various business functions. Traditionally, the focus has been on the vertical business functions, but I believe in shining a spotlight on the horizontal processes, breaking the functional barriers to allow the "water" to flow.

By mapping out these processes, we gained valuable insights into the bigger business pictures. We could clearly see how various business functions contributed to the overall customer experience. We could identify bottlenecks, streamline operations, and ensure every step aligned with customer-centric objectives.

Process mapping became the foundation of our organization's success.

It brought clarity, collaboration, and efficiency to our operations.

Process mapping is not just about creating static documents, it's about fostering a customer-centric mindset and continuously improving our processes to deliver exceptional value to customers.

A - Accountability Assignment

In the early days, I held myself accountable for every business process. I understood first-hand the significance of delighting customers because their satisfaction impacted our profitability and happiness. I took on the sole responsibility of achieving exceptional customer experiences.

However, as our organization grew, the dynamics changed. People in my organization were stationed within the "four walls" of their respective functional departments, often distanced from direct customer interactions.

This raised a critical question: How could they truly empathize with the challenges and pains of our customers, just as I did? How could we align everyone's efforts and propel the organization forward together, like a school of small fishes swimming in unison to resemble a giant fish?

Accountability Assignment, the "A" in PACKS, involves assigning a dedicated process owner who is accountable for the entire customer-centric process, spanning across multiple functional areas. This process owner serves as the bridge between our organization and our customers. There are many business processes, so there are many process owners.

The key aspect of this accountability is that it is customer result-driven, not merely focused on individual effort. The process owner becomes the driving force behind the process, ensuring that it aligns with customer business objectives, meeting and exceeding customer expectations, operating smoothly and efficiently, and driving desired outcomes.

By having a dedicated individual who is responsible for the entire process, we bridged the functional silos that can hinder collaboration and moved everyone in the same direction. This approach fosters a sense of shared responsibility, unity, and a collective commitment to our customers' success.

C - Cross-Functional Team

I encountered a situation where a team member didn't want to follow the process owner's guidance, saying "He is not my boss." It became clear to me that the process owner, while accountable for the customer-centric process, was not enabled because he did not hold the direct line management authority over the individuals involved. Each team member still reported to their respective functional leaders or department heads, who have their own set of priorities that may supersede the process owner's agenda.

To overcome these challenges, I implemented a formal cross-functional team, inviting key individuals from each functional area to join. In this matrix organization, the vertical structure of business functions remains intact, while a dynamic dotted-line cross-functional team structure emerges horizontally, led by the process owner. Each member is now also measured and incentivized by the results of process performance, with a clear focus on delivering exceptional value to our customers.

Cross-functional team, the "C" in PACKS, adds dynamics to our organization to embrace the ever-changing business environments. We were able to leverage the strengths and expertise of individuals across different functions in the business processes. The "walls" of functional silos become transparent if not broken down, enhancing collaborations, promoting a holistic understanding of the entire customer journey, and creating a shared sense of responsibilities.

It allows us to address customer needs more effectively and respond swiftly to the fast-changing business environments. Our organization becomes more adaptable, responsive, and capable of delivering superior customer experiences, leading to our success of building a top solar brand. We unlock new possibilities.

A cross-functional team is not just about an organization structure, a matrix drawing on paper. It is a mindset shift that embraces collaboration, shared accountability, and a relentless focus on customer satisfaction. By harnessing the collective talents and knowledge of members in the business organizations, we can achieve remarkable results and stay ahead in an ever-evolving business landscape.

K - KPI Measurement

As we formed our cross-functional team on this new journey, questions arose from team members:

"How do I know if I'm doing a good job?"

"How would you, as my manager, assess my performance?"

These questions also reflect the team's eagerness to understand their impacts.

Our after-sales service process often began when a customer contacted us, by phone call, email, or social media, reporting a product failure on-site. In this case, the service manager assumes the role of process owner, coordinating with the product team and design engineers to identify root causes, with service engineers for diagnoses, onsite or remotely, to explore solutions to solve problems quickly.

"What gets measured, gets done," a saying attributed to management guru Peter Drucker, is borrowed here.

Key Performance Indicators (KPIs) are a vital tool to gauge the success or failure of our processes in driving revenue and delighting customers for our business, like a thermometer in a room.

I designed the after-service process KPIs such as first contact response time and overall service time.

I designed regular reports, generated weekly and monthly, to monitor progress against KPI targets.

The purpose of defining KPIs is twofold.

First, they provide a means to objectively evaluate the performance of individuals. By setting clear expectations and measurable targets, team members gain a sense of direction and purpose.

Second, KPIs enable us, as leaders, to assess the effectiveness of our customer-centric process, providing valuable insights into areas of improvement.

By measuring customer-centric process performance through KPIs, we create a culture of accountability and continuous improvement. It fosters transparency and enables us to identify bottlenecks, inefficiencies, or areas where additional resources may be needed.

KPIs are not just numbers on a spreadsheet. They are powerful tools that guide our actions, align our efforts, and measure our success in creating exceptional customer experiences.

S - Share Knowledge

I established weekly internal knowledge sharing workshops. Pulling in people from across our cross-functional teams was initially met with some reluctance, but these workshops created a safe and inclusive environment where team members could share their expertise, insights, and perspectives, watching nodding heads and feeling admiring gazes from their peers. Everyone became actively involved in sharing, and it became a source of pride.

We might have experienced moments of frustration when trying to convey our ideas to others. This is natural, we are unique individuals with diverse backgrounds, experiences, and ways of thinking. We may use different language to express similar ideas or have varying interpretations of the same meanings, such as "making money" versus "becoming profitable." We complain that others don't understand us, and do not resonate with our perspective. Poor collaboration is the result.

Recognizing these differences, we acknowledge that it is neither practical nor feasible for everyone to be a jack-of-all-trades. However, we still want to harness the power of collective knowledge and learn to bridge these gaps and foster collaboration, leading to enhanced creativity and cost savings.

Sharing Knowledge in our PACKS organization strategy helps us create a nice team learning environment.

By actively listening and seeking to understand one another in the knowledge sharing workshops, we can cultivate a deeper appreciation for each other's ideas. This mutual understanding and trust is the foundation for effective collaboration and synergy.

It is essential, however, to exercise caution and protect confidential information during these knowledge sharing sessions. Strike the right balance between sharing knowledge and safeguarding sensitive information.

Knowledge is not meant to be hoarded or held tightly within silos. It is a valuable resource that becomes even more powerful when shared and disseminated across our organizations. We unlock the collective wisdom of our teams, maximize our potential, foster a culture of continuous learning and improvement, position our organization as an industry leader, and deliver exceptional value to our customers.

"ADDED" Dynamic Projects

"You put people together that have different skills, that look at the world differently ... and it is amazing what can come out of it."

— Tim Cook, Apple CEO

I spent a year in Singapore, working on the Accenture SAP Asian Rollout project for a Fortune 500 company. I enjoyed my time working with over sixty management consultants from more than ten countries, and tasting delicious foods from each country. This project was one of the first global digital transformation initiatives. I was fascinated by the diverse perspectives and skill sets that each team member brought to the table. We learned from one another, accelerating our product delivery timelines in ten Asian countries. We also enjoyed sightseeing in different countries together.

Throughout my years of business observations, I have come to believe that a forward-looking and self-renewing organization can thrive by operating within two parallel structures.

The first is a traditional organization structure consisting of clearly defined, well-run functional areas such as finance, products, sales, operation and supply chain, etc. These horizontal functional areas are interconnected by vertical customer-centric business processes, a matrix, an auspicious knot.

The second is an add-on, a dynamic and cross-functional project-based structure. This structure allows the organization to embark on short-term business initiatives that push the boundaries and prepare for the future, a green leaf swinging in the wind.

The "ADDED" dynamic project structure embraces the ever-changing business environment, allowing us to quickly seize potential opportunities. By fostering a culture of exploration, businesses can stay young.

I "ADDED" a project, a "How-to" training video series production to teach several hundred solar installers nationwide how to correctly and effectively install and service our newly launched solar inverter products. I named the project team the "Four-leaf clover." A four-leaf clover is widely considered a symbol of good luck, often associated with the rarity of good fortune, and also represents faith, hope, and love.

There are five steps to successfully execute this project:
A – Assemble Team
D – Define Objectives
D – Diversify Ideas
E – Execute with Freedom
D – Deliver and Share

A - Assemble Team

I assembled a diverse, multi-functional team that was ready to tackle the project.

I invited Bill as the lead instructor, a nationwide respected solar electrical code expert and educator. His expertise and credibility lent a strong foundation to the success of our educational videos. I selected three of our talented engineers to join the team, each possessing unique yet complementary skill sets. One was a product expert. Another was experienced with solar standards. The third was familiar with solar installations, and knew how to connect emotionally with solar installers. I was the executive sponsor, providing guidance and support, also ensuring there was a collaborative and cohesive team approach.

D - Define Objectives

Working closely with solar installers over the years, I gained deep insights into their specific needs.

It helped me define clear project objectives: to create engaging installation videos that solve installation problems quickly and easily, and to establish strong emotional connections with our installers. We sought to provide valuable service support and enhance the overall installer experience.

We aimed to develop short, fast-paced, 3-5-minute videos that were easy to search, which enabled installers to quickly access the information they needed to solve installation problems on-site.

D - Diversify Ideas

I organized brainstorming sessions for the team. Everyone was encouraged to contribute their ideas freely, regardless of hierarchy or seniority. Even the youngest engineer spoke out. This approach allowed us to tap into the diverse perspectives and experiences within the team, fostering collaborative open communication, where innovative ideas could flow freely.

E - Execute with Freedom

The team was given freedom to choose short video topics and execute the project according to their expertise and interests. Empowering the project team was crucial to harnessing their creativity and passion.

This approach not only fostered a sense of ownership and pride among the team members but also encouraged a joyful and enthusiastic approach to their work.

The product manager in the team sent me a picture of them painting the wall for mounting our solar equipment. The imagery of Tom Sawyer painting fences joyfully surfaced in my mind.

Installers could sense this positive energy while watching the videos, enhancing their loyal connection to our solar brand. They viewed our videos tens of thousands of times.

D - Deliver and Share

With the project completed, all project team members passionately shared these short training videos to reach as many installers as possible. We also featured them in our service portal. Many people, including from overseas, came to watch. These videos were disseminated widely, flying free on white wings, reaching out to thousands of people in the solar industry.

This widespread distribution of our videos extended our reach, surprisingly, providing valuable knowledge and compassionate support to solar installers, one of the key factors for helping us win the top solar brand award.

Build Trust: Reliability in "PCS"

On a sunny day, I walked out of Sunrun's office in a modern, tall building. Standing on the bustling Market Street in San Francisco, I found myself grappling with a question that held the key to our qualification for doing nationwide business with our top customer, Sunrun, a leading residential solar installer in the nation.

"What does Bankability mean?"

I was just told by the strategic sourcing director of Sunrun, that we must be bankable before being considered as one of their potential suppliers. But I don't even understand the meaning of the word, "Bankability".

I delved into the extensive questionnaire sent to me by DNV GL, a global quality assurance firm, providing expert advisory services, trusted by top financial institutions.

Understanding Bankability is made simpler by tracking the flow of money through the supply chain. In the solar industry, banks provide financing to solar installers, who in turn purchase solar equipment from manufacturers. Customers receive solar services from these installers under financial agreements such as Power Purchase Agreements (PPA), leasing, loans, or cash payments. The solar systems generate power, customers pay installers, and installers repay banks. Banks desire solar equipment to function reliably over an extended period, with minimal failure rates, in other words, more uptime. Their goals are a good return on investment and certainty of paybacks with minimum risks, just as we humans aspire to live long, healthy lives.

One word emerged in front of my eyes as a crucial clue: Reliability. "Reliability" blinks in the big stacks of documents I gathered to answer the DNV GL's extensive questionnaire to evaluate our "Bankability".

I summarized "Reliability" on three essential aspects: PCS.

P – Product Reliability
C – Company Reliability
S – Service Reliability

P - Product Reliability

Product reliability is not only about products.

Product reliability stems from the core values of a company, covering three key areas:
- Design for Reliability
- Manufacturing for Reliability
- Supply Chain for Reliability

Product reliability lab data only reflects half the story. It is the field performance of the products that truly matters—the real test of reliability in the real world, which is only visible in the long run.

The company culture of product reliability is cultivated when the entrepreneur constantly puts reliability first in the decision-making.

C - Company Reliability

Over the years, numerous solar manufacturers have disappeared from the solar market, leaving behind a trail of issues such as the unavailability of replacement parts or declining power production of solar equipment. Such instances tarnish the reputation of the solar industry, making top banks and big customers worried and cautious. They conduct due diligence when evaluating solar equipment manufacturers, seeking to partner with sustainable and profitable businesses with reliable products and great growth potential—business partners who will weather storms, both minor and severe, alongside them.

Company Reliability demonstrates a business's potential for long-term partnerships.

S - Service Reliability

Despite industry-leading reliability, inverters can occasionally fail. Big customers and top banks seek to partner with solar inverter manufacturers with reliable service. To meet their expectations, we invested in world-class service support infrastructure ahead of the curve. We assembled an experienced service team, implemented a cutting-edge, cloud-based CRM system, streamlined service processes, and developed a robust knowledge database. Our commitment to service reliability delights our customers, large or small, with a seamless experience.

Service Reliability showcases a business's capability to provide reliable services over extended periods.

Harmonious Operational Systems

Once, I attended Lang Lang's piano concert in Cincinnati. His fingers swiftly glided over the keys, like birds skimming the water's surface—fast yet exquisite.

I have come across numerous enterprises, big and small, with efficient operations. Their efficiency is not just about the visible speed.

The following points illustrate the underlying logic of efficient operations:

First, efficient operations are supported by an exquisitely designed and well-run operational system. It's akin to the music masters' scores that Lang Lang constantly referred to during his piano performances. A great operational system is systematic and comprehensive, with its various components coordinated and resonating with each other.

Second, efficiency is achieved through continuously refining the operational system over time. Lang Lang is disciplined, practicing piano rigorously day and night, repeating seemingly mundane movements. No operational system is perfect from the outset; rather, it is developed through day-to-day rectifying, improving the iterative business operations and processes.

Third, efficiency is maximized in maintaining elegant operational rhythms and cadence. Watching Lang Lang playing the piano, we immerse ourselves in the beautiful melodies of the music. Often, many businesses run in firefighting mode, requiring the business leaders to swiftly address sudden issues. While it might seem fulfilling for the business leaders to "show-off" their abilities to solve problems, it often leaves them exhausted, depleting their precious energy and dampening their spirits. Highly efficient enterprise operations have their own unique rhythm and cadence. The need for entrepreneurs to tackle unexpected problems is significantly reduced, with some being nipped in the bud and others resolved by the employees themselves.

Strategic Sourcing, Supplier Collaborations

"Values Blossom at the Interconnections Within the Business and Between Businesses."

– Susanna Huang

I used to lead large and complex strategic sourcing initiatives for Fortune 500 companies in the United States. These not only yielded an average of 10% to 20% cost savings, but more importantly, they achieved great value creations and operation efficiencies.

Strategic sourcing is the process of finding the right business partners to drive success and achieve strategic objectives. It involves a comprehensive approach to maximizing value across the supply chain, between a customer and its suppliers, reflecting the nature of interconnections.

Collaboration is a key driver of business effectiveness and efficiency, as it has a ripple effect in the supply chain. It is best achieved by looking for opportunities beyond traditional business boundaries.

By understanding the key steps in strategic sourcing strategy, you will potentially unlock the superpower in your business within your supply chain.

Spend Analysis - Unlocking Savings Opportunities
The first step is conducting a thorough spend analysis. By aggregating spend data from various locations with our local suppliers, we can identify and prioritize high-spend commodity categories across locations and uncover big potential savings opportunities for the business.

Request for Information (RFI) - Engaging Potential Suppliers

The next step is to research the industry and invite potential suppliers to participate in a Request for Information (RFI) initiative. The RFI helps gather essential information about the suppliers' capabilities, offerings, and suitability for the organization's needs. I suggest keeping the RFI questions concise and focused to encourage maximum participation while obtaining valuable insights into the related industry.

Request for Proposal (RFP): Crystallizing Objectives

The Request for Proposal (RFP) stage is where strategic sourcing objectives and requirements are crystallized. Through interviews with internal stakeholders, we define the major goals of the strategic sourcing projects, which typically include cost reduction, operation improvements, and value-added services. Creativity and innovations play vital roles in this stage, as we encourage suppliers to provide innovative ideas and solutions that align with our strategic objectives. The RFP is carefully designed with weighted scoring sections to ensure fair evaluation and selection.

Value Added Services: Unleashing the Power of Collaboration

Let us do a visualization exercise together. Imagine you put two organizations into one huge bubble, so they seem to be merged into one big organization. Would you be able to eliminate some overlapping business functions and streamline some processes?

The potential for value-added services is often overlooked.

For a large corporation with multiple locations and a wide geographic coverage, a centralized procurement strategy delivers value through optimizing the information flow, material flow, and money flow within the supply chain, yielding significant cost savings and improved operational efficiency.

1) Information flow: Before, each plant made local purchasing decisions from their local suppliers, managing the order-to-pay process, some were done manually. After our strategic sourcing project, a national supplier was awarded the business. They automated the order-to-pay processes and implemented a warehouse management system, freeing up our local effort. Leveraging suppliers' capabilities, our customer's local operations dramatically improved nationwide, with minimum cost.
2) Material flow: Before, each plant owned their local stock. After our strategic sourcing project, the supplier owned the stock, even though it was still located in the same plant. The cash tied to the inventory was freed up. Inventory carrying cost, calculated as the 30% of the stock value per rule of thumb, was saved.
3) Money flow: Before, each plant made its own local purchasing decisions. The payment term was short, like 15 or 30 days. After our strategic sourcing project, a much longer payment term was negotiated with the big national supplier, leveraging the negotiation power from aggregated corporate spend, and delivering more savings.

Once the new supplier program is established, we set up periodic account reviews with the strategic supplier. We review the cost savings achievements, new value-added service opportunities, etc. That's how I help clients build long-term strategic relationships with suppliers as a strategic sourcing consultant.

By shifting our focus from individual organizations to the collaborative power of the businesses in the supply chain, we can discover creative solutions, and uncover opportunities for delivering additional value at reduced costs, with improved service. Three seemingly conflicting goals achieved at the same time.

7 Reasons for Bringing Outsourcing to Insourcing

I worked closely with Fortune 500 companies to design and implement effective outsourcing strategies.

While outsourcing offers significant advantages, it is important to strike a balance between outsourcing and maintaining internal capabilities.

Outsourcing is a widely adopted business practice aimed at saving costs and mitigating risks by entrusting specific functions or processes to external providers. Businesses can tap into the expertise and infrastructure of these outsourcing partners, allowing themselves to focus on core competencies and strategic priorities.

In our solar business, I also outsourced the overflow of our service call center capacities. Outsourcing is particularly prevalent in the IT industry, with call centers being a prime example.

Successful outsourcing requires careful consideration and meticulous planning. It is essential to evaluate potential outsourcing partners based on their expertise, track record, and cultural fit.

Sometimes, we want to bring outsourced operations back in-house. Insourcing is focusing on building internal excellence. Here are seven reasons for insourcing, bringing outsourced operations in-house.

Reason 1: Core Business Operations
Reason 2: Cost Considerations
Reason 3: Collaboration Challenges
Reason 4: Ethical Concerns
Reason 5: Evolving Business Requirements
Reason 6: Clouded Communications
Reason 7: Your Gut Feelings

Reason 1: Core Business Operations

It is crucial to identify and retain control over core business operations. Each organization has unique value propositions that set them apart from competitors. Core functions, whether it's a unique brand strategy, a cost-efficient supply chain infrastructure, or top-class global service capabilities, should be nurtured internally. By recognizing what truly defines our core business capabilities, we can determine which operations should NOT be considered for outsourcing. Rather than outsourcing it, we would insource it.

Reason 2: Cost Considerations

Outsourcing decisions are often driven by cost analyses that show potential savings. However, it is important to periodically conduct regular cost analyses to help determine the optimal approach. Factors such as market conditions, business growth, and stability can influence cost dynamics over time. For instance, during periods of rapid growth, outsourcing may be a cost-effective solution to manage variable workloads. As the business stabilizes, it may be more financially prudent to bring outsourced operations in-house.

Reason 3: Collaboration Challenges

Over time, collaboration issues may arise with outsourcing suppliers, leading to frustration and unfulfilled requests. While communication issues can be resolved, collaboration issues can drain our energy and hinder progress. Even if cost savings are apparent, it may be beneficial to bring the outsourced operation back in-house. Outsourcing should not impede the overall efficiency and effectiveness of the business.

Reason 4: Ethical Concerns

Ethical issues with an outsourcing supplier can have detrimental effects on our business reputation. Encroachments on business property, spreading untruthful messages, or overcharging for services are examples of ethical concerns that should not be taken lightly. While it may be difficult to sever ties with a supplier still providing necessary services, preserving our business reputation takes precedence. Upholding ethical standards is essential, and in such cases, insourcing becomes the preferred option.

Reason 5: Evolving Business Requirements

As a business evolves, so do the requirements. The scope of work defined with an outsourced supplier may no longer align with our changing business needs. It is crucial to periodically reassess the scope of work and evaluate whether it adequately supports our business growth and objectives. If the scope of work dramatically shifts, it may be time to bring the operation in-house or seek a new outsourcing partner that aligns with our evolving requirements.

Reason 6: Clouded Communications

Outsourcing may inadvertently hinder direct communication with customers, preventing us from promptly addressing customer complaints, understanding product issues, or gaining valuable insights. These communication barriers can impede our ability to protect our business interests and maintain customer relationships. When our own communication channels are compromised, insourcing becomes a safer option to regain control and foster direct customer engagement.

Reason 7: Trusting Your Gut Feelings

Sometimes, despite careful analysis, our intuition or "gut feelings" can guide us in the right direction. Taking the time to listen to our inner voice, whether during a mindfulness moment in nature or in meditation, can provide valuable insights. By honing our intuitions through practices, we can develop a stronger sense of what decisions align with our best interests.

In summary, outsourcing is not always the optimal strategy.

In the above cases, insourcing is the right strategy.

Change is Constant.

Personal Transformation is a Business Strategy

"Be Systematic. Be Holistic. Be Poetic."

– Susanna Huang

Now, I invite you to embark on a transformative journey. Find a quiet place where you can immerse yourself fully. Take a piece of paper, fold it in half, and open it up. Write "Yesterday" in the top-left corner and "Tomorrow" in the top-right corner.

On the left side, under "Yesterday," quickly jot down your old knowledge, old skills, old beliefs, old social circles, and old identities. Now, take a moment to reflect and carefully examine each item on the left side. With a stroke of the pen, cross out the things from the past that no longer serve you. Just as spring-cleaning clears away the clutter, letting go of what no longer aligns with your newly found life purposes will alleviate your worries and create space for new possibilities, filling you with new energy.

As you turn your attention to the right side of the paper, under "Tomorrow," you will find ample space to gradually write down new knowledge, new skills, new beliefs, new social circles, and new identities.

In the world of entrepreneurship, where challenges, opportunities, and uncertainties abound, personal transformation becomes an integrated part of our business journey, a catalyst for our long-term success. Entrepreneurs can stay ahead of the curve by making wise business decisions and courageously seizing emerging opportunities. This willingness to evolve and change oneself allows entrepreneurs to navigate the ever-changing business landscape with resilience and determination.

Entrepreneurs who embrace personal transformation develop the inner strength to bounce back and persevere in the face of adversity. They understand that setbacks and obstacles are not roadblocks but rather steppingstones on the path to success. Like a phoenix rising from the ashes, they rise stronger and more determined after each challenge.

Furthermore, personal transformation enhances an entrepreneur's leadership capabilities. As global leadership guru John Maxwell eloquently put it, "Leadership ability is the lid that determines a person's level of effectiveness." By continuously growing and evolving, entrepreneurs and business leaders expand their leadership potential, effectively inspiring and guiding their teams to achieve greatness.

In the realm of entrepreneurship, personal transformation is not just a luxury—it is a necessity. It empowers entrepreneurs to adapt and thrive. It equips us with the proper mindsets and tools. And navigating the complexities of entrepreneurship helps us make a lasting impact on our businesses and the world around us.

7 Most Important Questions

Personal transformation begins with self-reflection and self-discovery, exploring the precious moments that have shaped our lives and the transformative experiences that have led us to where we are today. In this journey of self-discovery, I present the 7 most important questions, designed to help us navigate our "Yesterday" with self-awareness and prepare us for the process of self-renewal in our "Tomorrow".

Allow me to share a glimpse of my own stories, along with these 7 most important questions, as we embark on this journey together.

Question Number 1: What attracted you to do what you enjoy doing today?

It all started when I heard our head of global sustainability share the story of solar's popularity in Germany, his home country. The magic of solar energy captivated my imagination and sparked a deep passion within me.

Question Number 2: How did you learn to rise to the top in your space?

My greatest lessons were learned through solving real-world problems. It was in those moments of practical applications that I truly excelled and honed my skills, reaching new heights in my space.

Question Number 3: What was your biggest a-ha moment in life?

On a serene summer night, I gazed at the mesmerizing stars shimmering over the dark Pacific Ocean. Looking at the picture I took that night, an a-ha moment struck me. It was in that instant that I conceived the idea for the 7 Stars Global Solar Education Guide.

Question Number 4: How do you connect with people?

My preferred approach is to collaborate with professionals from diverse disciplines on shared projects. By leveraging the collective wisdom and expertise of others, we can create something truly remarkable and impactful.

Question Number 5: What is your biggest lesson learned?

Through introspection, I have come to realize the importance of operating within my strength zone, which I affectionately refer to as my "genius zone." While it is easy to remain in comfort zones, true growth comes from embracing our unique strengths while venturing into new territories.

Question Number 6: What will be your next big move?

My vision is to attract exceptional talents to join our Enso Circle Space—an environment where we can learn from the best, share with our peers, grow in a nurturing atmosphere, and contribute to our communities to collectively achieve greatness in the business world.

Question Number 7: What legacy would you like to leave on our lovely planet?

My aspiration is to illuminate the world with the love and light of solar energy, spreading joy, peace, and happiness in harmony with nature, while addressing the challenges of climate change.

As you explore these 7 most important questions, may they serve as guideposts on your path of personal growth and transformation. Embrace the insights you uncover when you answer these questions, and let them shape your journey as you strive to make a meaningful impact on yourself, your business, and the world.

7 Common Learning Mistakes to Avoid

"The only real mistake is the one from which we learn nothing."

- Henry Ford

We find ourselves living in a whole new world, facing countless unknowns and uncertainties. In this ever-evolving landscape, our willingness to unlearn what we know and continuously embrace new learning becomes paramount for our survival and prosperity. It is the key to seizing new opportunities and charting a new course towards a brighter future.

At any given moment, we have the power to choose our path. We can either continue on the familiar road we've been traveling, or we can make a conscious decision to forge a new path, right here and right now. We want to create the right causes and conditions for our new journeys.

Today, I want to share with you seven common mistakes that many people, including myself, have made. Perhaps some of these mistakes resonate with you. If so, I urge you to avoid these pitfalls as you embark on your new journey. By recognizing these traps early on, you can navigate towards your life purposes and illuminate your path with the brilliance of your true self.

There are seven sections in this chapter, each dedicated to exploring a specific mistake that may hinder your ability to shine your brightest light. But fear not, for in each section, I also offer a pathway to transform these mistakes into valuable lessons.

Every mistake is an opportunity for growth and learning.

Mistake #1: No Longer Learning Proactively

Many of us have invested heavily in formal education, some taking on substantial student loans to pursue our academic goals. However, as we grow older, the demands of daily family life and work responsibilities gradually consume our precious time.

How often do we choose to relax and indulge in entertainment rather than dedicate time to learning? It seems that not many of us prioritize ongoing education. We can easily find numerous reasons to justify our lack of learning, such as expensive tuition fees, long travel distances to educational institutions, and the time-consuming nature of classes. Our brains are skilled at supporting our arguments, right or wrong.

But have you ever wondered how some people manage to continue learning and growing despite having similar circumstances? How can they then enjoy long, fulfilling, and rewarding careers?

As a lifelong learner with busy schedules and frequent travel commitments, I embarked on a quest to discover new ways of incorporating learning into my daily life. Learning becomes more than just an occasional pursuit—it became a lifestyle for new humans.

And that's when I stumbled upon the concept of "bite-size" learning. Instead of committing to lengthy training sessions or courses, I discovered the power of breaking down learning into manageable chunks that easily fit into the gaps of my busy schedule. For example, fascinating research by Dr. Paul Kelley revealed that intense 20-minute bursts of study, interspersed with 10-minute breaks, can lead to better long-term memory retention compared to longer, uninterrupted study periods.

Let me share some examples of my bite-size learning experiences. I would listen to course recordings while jogging in the woods, watch educational videos on my iPhone while waiting for a plane to arrive, or read a few pages of a book while enjoying a cup of coffee at a local café. These small, consistent efforts added up and made a significant impact on my knowledge acquisition, personal growth, and transformation.

Bite-size learning is a highly effective approach in the modern age, as it allows us to fit education seamlessly into our busy lives. I have personally witnessed the tremendous benefits of this approach, and I encourage you to embark on your own bite-size learning journey to unlock your full potential and continue to grow.

Now is the time for you to embrace the concept of "learning how to learn."

Mistake #2: Not Having a Guide for Education

I'm curious how you developed an interest in your career?
    Did you follow your parent's advice?
    Did you listen to advice from your friends?
    Did you learn the subjects at college?
    Or did you study the industry before jumping in?

I knew very little about solar when I quit my comfortable big corporate job to join the budding solar industry. I tried to learn from everywhere, but got more confused each day with the overflow of information.

That was until I met an Accenture Alumnus who introduced me to Sunrun, the largest Home Solar and Storage Installer in the United States. With this top customer, I had a unique opportunity of working with a wide range of solar professionals, i.e., designers, banks, testing labs, standards organizations, training organizations, service people etc., accelerating my learning holistically and systematically.

A unique Seven (7) Stars Education Guide for the global solar professionals emerged in my mind in an a-ha moment when I was gazing at the mesmerizing stars shimmering over the dark Pacific Ocean. Like stars, the guide shows the roadmap for your personal development if you're interested in the solar industry. I am excited to share it with you later in this book. You may be surprised to see how solar energy is reshaping everyone's life. You may want to leapfrog and make a bigger impact on protecting our Mother Earth. If you're in other industries, I suggest you make a conscious effort to find an educational guide, while also learning about the framework of thinking from this guide.

Mistake #3: Not Knowing One's Own Genius

My parents helped me select my electrical engineering major for college.

I became a management consultant with Accenture after graduation.

I pursued an MBA, following in the footsteps of my Accenture colleagues.

But one day, I realized that I should make my own decisions for my life, my precious life.

I left the big Fortune 500 corporation and ventured into the solar industry.

So how about you? Are you working in the area where your parents pushed you, your friends recommended, or what your teachers told you to do? Or have you made your own choices?

How do you feel about working in your industry right now?

Is your work interesting or boring?
Is your job easy or difficult?
Do you feel your spirit is shining or dimmed?

Your feelings tell a lot about whether you're working in your strength zone. Contrary to the old suggestion of working on our weaknesses, I believe in working in our strength zone. Why? Because your competition is working in their strength zone. But, do you really know your own genius?

I had pictured myself as a scholar for a long time. One day, I visited our MBA career director, who told me I had good negotiation skills, my jaw almost dropped. But my later experience as a strategic sourcing consultant proved his point. You never know your genius unless you begin to doubt if you have ever really discovered your genius. Do not assume you have tapped into your full capabilities.

John Maxwell, a leadership guru I have followed for years, shared his suggestions in his article "Finding Your Own Strength Zone." 1. Ask, "What am I doing well?"; 2. Get Specific; 3. Listen to What Others Praise; 4. Check Out the Competition.

Mistake #4: Not Getting Fresh Knowledge

Sometimes, it is not easy to tell if what you learned is old knowledge or fresh knowledge. Old knowledge used to be the fresh knowledge, in the past. The cost of learning old knowledge could be high, impacting not only the time and effort you invested, but also the potential financial award of your future career opportunities.

Time for learning is precious. If you don't let go of the old knowledge consciously, you will not have enough mental space for the new.

How can you advance in your career faster while having the same time in the day as everyone else?

I discovered an easy path—learning from the best. You need to find out where the best source of knowledge to learn from can be found. I put more trust on fresh knowledge from the thought leaders in a particular space.

Our energy vibration could even be lifted higher by coming closer to these noble souls.

The best people I've encountered have all had profound impacts on my life, my precious life…

A speaker at a conference once told me that he learned from everyone. He said our life is like clay, and everyone we encountered left their unique prints on our clay of life.

In the past, we were restricted to living in our little corners of the world. It was not easy to have access to the best teachers, and thought leaders etc. That's not a big problem anymore today.

Mistake #5: Not Mastering Soft Skills

Have you ever wondered why a colleague got promoted, and not you?

Or why your friend landed a higher paying job?

Do you wonder why, even though you are a talented, hard worker, few people appreciate your effort?

I've asked these questions to myself as well. My career path has been full of ups and downs, like walking on the twists and turns of mountain trails.

The higher you climb the corporate ladders, the more important the soft skills. It sounds simple, but I learned from my own experience the hard way. I had a great start with my career because of my hard skills in engineering, but I suffered some career setbacks due to my ignorance of soft skills.

If you do a simple exercise of recording the time you spend on different career development tasks in a month, how much time do you allocate to improving your hard skills? And how much on soft skills, such as people engagement, presentation, networking, resume writing, negotiation, etc.? Are you allocating enough time to developing your soft skills?

Beyond the traditional soft skills, we also need to learn the fresh soft skills of the modern age. Mindfulness is a good one. In an article from Forbes, titled "Increasing Mindfulness in the Workplace" by Yolanda Lau, it says, "Mindfulness matters. The ability to be present and mindful—to stay focused intentionally without passing judgement—is a 21st century skill. Businesses with mindful teams are better equipped to compete in today's ever-changing environment."

It is up to us to set the right intention to learn soft skills.

Mistake #6: Neglecting Your Supportive Community

Who was happy for you when you received a career promotion? Signed a big contract? Who was with you to cheer you up when you were down after losing a business deal? Who shared their wisdom with you to help you advance in your career? Your family members may care about you, but they probably don't know your business well. Sometimes, you may not want to shift the burden of work to your loved ones. Out of concerns about competition, many people choose to keep things to themselves, happy or sad, instead of engaging others. It is why many of us felt loneliness or even depression during pandemic periods.

According to a global survey, about 33 percent of adults

experienced feelings of loneliness worldwide. I had the same concerns. We should be very careful about who we share with and what we share—and what not to share. In-person connections are what really matters, they help us mitigate and minimize loneliness.

So, wouldn't it be nice to have somebody who is on the same wavelength with us to discuss our business questions and concerns, probably hundreds of miles away in a safe online community environment?

Imagine if you get stuck on a question, you can ask this question in the community and get answers from other solar professionals, without spending hours searching for the right answer, sometimes you may even get wrong answers online without knowing it.

I believe that going global is better and easier than going local for meaningful interactions. We also get good feelings from helping a friend, which is also beneficial for our health, even if they live on another continent.

Mistake #7: Not Having a Higher Purpose

Are you still passionate about your career? Do you feel good about yourself after experiencing the many ups and downs in your career? Are you still hoping to stay in your industry even after being exhausted riding the career roller coasters?

From the time you graduated from high school, you have probably now earned more money and achieved a higher social status. Are you happier and more fulfilled than before?

Interestingly, happiness is not always tied to money and social status, though they are important.

Knowing our own inner goodness and having a personal higher purpose promotes our well-being and more lasting happiness.

I chose to work in the Solar industry because of the three bottom lines—social, environmental, and financial, with built-in higher purpose. No matter where we live on this planet, we are blessed with sunshine, and I feel we could work together to brighten the world with the love and light of solar energy. This belief brought me back to solar again and again after many career challenges. What is it that's special about your chosen field?

Read and Write

"Reading and writing intertwine in a graceful dance."

– Susanna Huang

My writing unexpectedly led me to some interesting places—working with Solar magazines in India and the US, the Eiffel Tower in Paris-France, Publishing House in London, and Solar businesses in San Francisco, California.

My passion for writing started from reading. I have been an avid reader since I was a kid, with books glued to my hands. But I'm now more selective, spending time on three main categories of books.

First, I delved into the biographies of great business leaders like Steve Jobs and personal transformation leaders like Marci Shimoff. These noble people shine light with their unique values, and resonate deeply within me. Through their life and business stories, I gain insights into their worldviews, which are shaped by their amazing experiences. I accompany them on their journeys through challenging situations, feeling their emotions, and witnessing their personal growth. I observe their decision-making, balancing multiple factors while staying true to their core values. Rereading these books feels like reconnecting with old friends. At times, the wisdom I absorb becomes an intuitive guide in solving challenging problems I faced.

Second, I explore modern business books. Facing the turbulent environment, I anticipate the significant shifts in the way business is conducted, while acknowledging that fundamental business principles remain unchanged. Absorbing fresh insights from new thought leaders motivates me to swiftly apply newfound knowledge to actions in business, where the real learning takes place.

Third, I delve into the world of the latest technologies. Although these academic readings can be dry, I find it beneficial to intersperse them between the more enjoyable categories mentioned above. By striking a balance, I ensure a well-rounded intake of information, the valuable practical knowledge used for business.

Yet, information intake through reading is only part of the equation. Information output through writing completes the learning cycle, creating a healthy and fulfilling circle of personal growth and transformation.

We learn, contemplate, and meditate until the knowledge enters our mind stream.

Writing is a form of meditation for me, a joyful inner journey of self-discovery.

I write continuously during my learning journey. As I penned my thoughts and ideas, a profound realization unfolded—I was illuminating the shadows of my unconsciousness. Writing shines the light on my inner self, sometimes unknown, and new creative ideas surface gracefully from nowhere. This is how I unveiled the Enso's Inner House of Business Framework in this *Little Stone Lion* business book.

Reading and writing intertwine in a graceful dance.

Through reading, I absorbed fresh knowledge and gained valuable perspectives.

Through writing, I opened my mind to new spaces, deepened my self-awareness, and unlocked hidden potentials.

May each page we turn and each word we pen bring us closer to our true selves, empowering us to make a lasting impact on our lives, businesses, and the world around us.

Reading and writing are among the most effective tools for self-discovery and personal transformation.

Chasing Knowledge like "CATS"

"Chasing CATS: Create, Apply, Teach, Share Knowledge."

– Susanna Huang

From a young age, I embraced the belief that "Knowledge is Power."

But is this still true?

Tony Robbins, a thought leader, reminds us that "Knowledge is NOT power. Knowledge is only POTENTIAL power. Action is power."

I was a young Accenture consultant fresh out of Tsinghua University when I sought ways to rapidly expand my knowledge and present myself professionally to clients, top brands. Thankfully, Accenture had a global knowledge base, a treasure trove of insights contributed by talented consultants from around the world. I eagerly "borrowed" knowledge from there, arming myself with confidence before meeting clients.

I want to challenge the traditional notion of safeguarding knowledge that some individuals accumulate over the years. Today, knowledge is readily available at our fingertips, and it becomes obsolete quickly. Instead of focusing solely on the acquisition of knowledge, we want to shift our attention towards gaining valuable insights from the knowledge and applying that knowledge in the fields more quickly and effectively.

When I contemplate on the lifecycle of knowledge, I imagine the fun image of cats chasing their tails—a perpetual cycle that consists of Create, Apply, Teach, and Share knowledge.

C – Create Knowledge
A – Apply Knowledge
T – Teach Knowledge
S – Share Knowledge

C – Create Knowledge

I created a comprehensive Knowledge Base for our business. Imagine walking through the aisles of a bookstore, selecting books to read. Our Knowledge Base serves like a bookstore, housing our best practices and insights for people, both internally and externally, and promoting effective and efficient learnings.

Traditionally, individuals carried knowledge in their heads from one place to another, job to job.

"Creating knowledge" is maybe better described as "Downloading knowledge" from people's minds into our Knowledge Base. This endeavor required significant effort. I assigned one subject-matter expert to each knowledge area, who would then coordinate the transfer of people's expertise to the Knowledge Base, freeing up their precious mental space for fresh learning. This process, which I also called "unlearning," facilitated quick learning for our team members, fostering graceful flows of information, and helping the new learning by others.

A - Apply Knowledge

By applying knowledge proactively, our subject-matter experts became adept at using knowledge more effectively in their jobs. This exercise deepened their understanding and sharpened their thinking, enabling them to creatively solve business problems.

Knowledge must flow and come alive to exhibit its power. If left sitting on a shelf, knowledge merely collects dust, akin to countless papers in university libraries. Knowledge possesses power when applied in our daily work and life, like flowing water.

T - Teach Knowledge

I implemented weekly internal knowledge exchange workshops, encouraging our subject-matter experts to teach their peers. These workshops fostered team engagement and dynamic discussions, creating a collective learning experience for everyone involved. Knowledge gains power when it is taught, and also enhances the understanding of the teacher. As a result, our teams grew closer, functioning as a unified force, and brought many creative and innovative solutions to our customers.

S - Share Knowledge

I organized monthly webinars where we shared our expertise with our customers, often co-hosted with industry-leading experts. Our target audience, mostly solar installers nationwide, had the opportunity to learn from the very best, the source of industry-specific knowledge, elevating our brand and fostering trusting relationships with our customers. Subject-matter experts felt honored to collaborate with the industry leaders, who they admired and respected, making it a profound learning experience for all involved. Knowledge exerts its power when it is shared.

Wonderful Passions

In our early days, people showed little interest in our solar inverters, a little-known brand, even when we offered them as free samples.

However, one encounter changed everything.

I walked into the office of a prominent solar installer in California, graciously welcomed by David, the owner. Midway through my presentation, he interrupted me and expressed his willingness to purchase. As a new salesperson, I insisted on finishing my pitch, but David insisted that I had already convinced him to buy.

It was through the energy of my passion that we broke the ice and established a business relationship.

While knowledge is undoubtedly important, it is passion that truly resonates with people on an energetic level. Whether meeting face to face or connecting remotely, passion has the power to forge deep connections.

Passion has worked wonders for our business in numerous cases.

During a solar conference in Mexico, an unexpected opportunity arose when I shared the founder's entrepreneurship story, which is quite inspiring. I spoke about how our inverter business originated in a dorm during his Ph.D. studies, and how customers approached us at trade shows to express their appreciation for our reliable products. One of SolarCity's executives was touched by my passion and introduced me to their procurement director in their headquarters in California. This ultimately led to the procurement and installation of our solar inverters at SolarCity, the largest solar installer at the time with one third of the US residential market share, which was later acquired by Tesla.

Passion can be cultivated through pure intention and

having genuine enthusiasm.

People can sense your passion, and they naturally gravitate towards individuals who embody it.

I encourage you to discover your passion and let it shine through when interacting with others, to forge genuine connections at the human level and fuel your journey towards success.

Susanna Qiang Huang

Minority and Introvert? So Be It.

"Remain true to yourself."

– Susanna Huang

During my time at Fisher College of Business at The Ohio State University, I struggled with MBA social events. The pressure to attend these events caused headaches and even discomfort in my throat. I contemplated avoiding them altogether, but I was concerned about losing job opportunities: Thankfully, I still managed to secure a desirable consulting job before graduation—without going to bars.

As a minority and introvert, I have gained unique insights into personal transformation, especially in the United States, a country predominantly populated by extroverts.

The first lesson I learned is to embrace my authentic self, pursuing my genuine interests. I wasn't the only outlier in my class. One of my MBA classmates from India was passionate about investments, and would often share his thoughts during class, frequently quoting his idol, Warren Buffett. While some classmates would laugh, he remained unfazed and continued sharing his insights. We all grew to appreciate him. This experience also taught me to not be deterred by the opinions of others, and remain true to myself.

The second lesson I learned was the power of focusing on making people connections rather than obsessing over my own imperfect grammar or pronunciation when I speak English, my second language. When I shifted my attention to genuinely understanding and connecting with people, my nerves subsided, and the right words effortlessly flowed from my mind to my mouth. The delivery became fantastic, forming meaningful connections. People also began to appreciate my unique accent.

The third lesson I learned was the importance of finding a role model. After my MBA graduation, I joined a leading management consulting firm, later acquired by Accenture. It was an exciting opportunity, but I also felt nervous about working alongside talented native consultants. I had the privilege of working with a Vietnam-born manager who graduated from Oxford with a mathematics degree, and who formerly worked at a prestigious management consulting firm. Despite being a quiet introvert with a Vietnamese accent, he commanded respect within the firm due to his strategic thinking and his willingness to mentor young professionals. His authenticity and success inspired me, as I could envision myself thriving in the U.S. business environment. And I did.

Embrace your uniqueness. Let it be your source of strength and perspective.

Susanna Qiang Huang

Poetry, Beyond Passion

"The Intersection of Art and Technologies is Where Magic Happens."

– Susanna Huang

"Poetry is like a delicate flower, blossoming from the depth of the soul."

– Susanna Huang

I'm passionate about poetry. I am so grateful to Black Spring Press Group, a respected poetry publisher in London, United Kingdom, who published Moon Creek, my collection of nature poetry.

For me, poetry is not a distant art form; it also serves as a source of healing and solace, my meditation walks in Nature. When I turned my attention inward and delved into my inner world, the beauty of nature was unveiled to me, which had a profound impact on my well-being and happiness.

Through a decade of meditation practice, I became attuned to my feelings and more aware of how the external environment affects my emotions. Just as a flower blooms in a nurturing environment, I realized that I thrive when I am in a positive state of emotions.

So, what might be the role of poetry in our businesses, beyond passion?

Let me start with one word: ChatGPT. While we may feel excitement and curiosity about ChatGPT, Elon Musk has expressed his belief that artificial intelligence could pose more danger than nuclear weapons. How can we navigate these potential risks? I believe the key lies in our ability to quickly transcend our human being selves and cultivate three essential qualities.

First, Empathy. An AI robot once mentioned that machines lack emotions, which distinguishes them from humans. On the other hand, poetry is like a delicate flower, blossoming from the depth of the soul. In a precious moment, poetry and humans create a magical emotional resonance. Reading poetry nourishes our empathy, enabling us to deeply connect with other human beings and nature.

Second, Creativity. While ChatGPT was intended to assist humans and take over repetitive tasks, there is understandable fear and worry about jobs that might be replaced by machine-like functions. Poetry, however, is a product of human creativity. It flows from one heart to another, transcending boundaries. Reading poetry cultivates our own creative abilities, allowing us to approach challenges in unique and imaginative ways, leading to more human opportunities.

Third, Imagination. Artificial intelligence focuses on learning and reasoning, but it lacks the imaginative capacity that humans possess. In the realm of poetry, the lines between imagination and reality blur, and disciplinary boundaries fade away, dreams merge with realities. It enables us to explore limitless possibilities, transcend time and space, and forge emotional connections with others. Reading poetry nurtures our imagination, expanding our perspectives and fostering innovative thinking.

Calm and Joyful at Meru Peak

I once had the opportunity to meet with one of the world's finest rock-climbers, explorers, photographers, and film directors.

Sitting at the front table, I happened to strike up a conversation with a young gentleman next to me. He told me his name was Jimmy Chin.

As a sponsor of solar inverters, I attended the national sales conference hosted by our major client, Sunrun, in San Diego. The dining room was full of excitement.

To my surprise, Jimmy Chin later took the stage. I realized he was the keynote speaker for the evening, invited by Sunrun to deliver an inspirational speech.

Both of Jimmy Chin's parents came from mainland China, and he is a second-generation Chinese-American.

Jimmy narrated his journey from being his parents' obedient son, a well-behaved student, to becoming a mountain climber challenging the world's most difficult rock walls.

His parents were very concerned about his reliance on rock climbing for a living, fearing he might go hungry and end up with no place to stay. And indeed, there was a time when he lived in a truck. However, his passion for extreme climbing endured.

During a financially challenging period, he resorted to selling his photographs for money, which unexpectedly led to him becoming a photographer for National Geographic magazine.

We listened to him recounting the thrilling ascent of the enigmatic Meru Peak, one of the most difficult and mysterious climbing experiences in the world. Watching the breathtaking climbing photographs of Meru Peak on the screen, we were all nervously holding our breath.

He refrained from using the commonly used word "conquer" when referring to the mountains, expressing instead a sense of reverence and love in his words.

A few months later, while watching the Oscars, I heard a familiar name announced as the winner of the Academy Award Winner for Best Documentary. I was astonished to see Jimmy Chin and his wife standing on the podium to receive the award.

I vividly recall Jimmy Chin's smiling remark during his speech at Sunrun that day:

Standing at the world's highest and most treacherous mountain peaks, he felt a sense of Joy and Peace.

Perhaps this could also be the beautiful dream state of our courageous entrepreneurs.

Susanna Qiang Huang

Unity in Human Communities, A Return to Paris

"We must ask ourselves a key question, what kind of world are we leaving for our future generations?"

- United Nations Secretary General António Guterres

In the summer of 2022, I returned to Paris, invited to speak at the Paris Sustainable Blockchain Summit.

Together with experts from around the world, we discussed how to address the climate change challenge. The Technical Officer—the United Nations Framework Convention on Climate Change (UNFCCC) secretariat—was also in attendance, speaking and mingling with us.

I shared my insights on solar energy data communication standards, as the board member of SunSpec.

I was deeply experiencing the enormous changes brought about by the latest technological advancements in the world. It was my first time intimately feel the warmth of "Unity in Human Communities". "DAO" – Way as called by Laozi, were frequently brought up by these world-class experts.

More questions began to surface in my mind, I reflected and contemplated on these questions.

What if the scarcity of energy on earth is just an illusion? There is abundant solar energy.

The Sun is shining unselfishly on the Himalaya mountains, on the Pacific Ocean, on commercial buildings, and on our rooftops, etc. Sunshine is everywhere on our planet.

Imagine if all the people under the sun could enjoy solar energy in Joy, Peace and Harmony.

If so, why do we not all have access to abundant solar

energy? I realized it was the perfect time for me to make a career move again, like a decade before.

As part of the human community, we must collectively address the decisive human crisis of climate change.

Being in the solar energy industry, I felt an even greater sense of mission.

I dedicate the following chapter to the solar energy industry, hoping to pique your interest and encourage your involvement. Sunshine is on everyone.

7 Stars Global Solar Education Guide

"Solving Real-world Business Problems with Sparks of Intuitions, not with Stacks of Books."

– Susanna Huang

"Imagination, Creativity, and Innovation flow into Purpose-Driven Businesses."

– Susanna Huang

Little Stone Lion

One summer night, after attending a solar conference in San Diego, I found myself alone, strolling into the enveloping darkness. The shimmering stars above cast their gentle light upon me, while the melodic whispers of the Pacific Ocean provided a serene backdrop.

Throughout history, when venturing into the unknown, people have looked up to the stars as their guiding compass. Inspired by this timeless practice, I decided to present the seven distinct areas within the realm of solar, using a simple, yet powerful analogy: B.E.S.T. Are For Stars — the 7 Stars Global Solar Education Guide, which will illuminate your path in Solar, helping our effort to face climate change challenges, and forge a brighter future for ourselves and generations to come. Solar is for everyone.

For nearly a decade, I have traversed the intricate landscape of the solar industry. Along the way, I have experienced the challenges and triumphs of solving real-world business problems. Now, I invite you to join me on a much easier and faster learning path to shine your own bright light.

In the vast ocean of solar information, I once found myself overwhelmed. However, an encounter with an Accenture alumnus paved the way for me to work with Sunrun, the number one home solar storage installer in the United States. Within Sunrun's vast network, I had the privilege of collaborating with a diverse range of solar professionals. From designers to banks, testing labs to standards organizations, training institutions to service providers. I immersed myself in the intricacies of the solar industry, including months spent delving deep into the complexities of a "bankability" study with DNV GL, ultimately leading to our recognition as an approved vendor for esteemed financial institutions, among one of few solar inverter manufacturers.

In this captivating chapter, I invite you to embark on a

transformative journey as we delve into the intricacies of the solar industry, as an illusory, unveiling invaluable insights that you can readily apply to your industry, even it is not solar. Together, we will explore the broader applications of Enso's Inner House of Business Framework—a remarkable tool that transcends boundaries, applied to various industries.

B.E.S.T. Are for Stars

Many people tend to focus solely on learning specific functional areas, most are fragmented. However, it is crucial to understand the interconnectedness of various areas. A holistic and systematic approach for learning an industry such as Solar is the key to unlocking our full potential.

I discovered the "B.E.S.T. Are for Stars" 7 Stars Solar Education Guide.

B.E.S.T. Are for Stars:

B – Business: Embrace a bird's-eye view of the solar industry, including the supply chain, enabling you to comprehend the intricate network of the business landscape in its entirety.

E – Equipment: Immerse yourself in the study of diverse solar equipment to gain comprehensive knowledge of solar systems and their components.

S – Standards & Regulations: Grasp the profound impact that industry standards and regulations have on solar adoption, transcending mere safety considerations.

T – Transformation: Embark on a personal journey of growth and transformation, nurturing the qualities of new relationships that will propel you toward success.

A – Applications: Explore solar applications worldwide, uncovering innovative ways in which solar energy can be harnessed to shape a sustainable future, collaboratively.

F – Financing: Harness the power of financing to unlock the immense potential of the solar market to better understand the impact of financing that drives its growth.

S – Service: Foster the design and construction of modern, reliable, efficient, and cost-effective service support infrastructure to ensure exceptional customer experience.

Each of these areas possesses its own expertise and unique learning path, and are accompanied by inspirational stories that will fuel your journey.

B - Business: Unleash Your Potentials

Visiting Sunrun, I engaged in various discussions with their talented solar professionals in a conference room that offered breathtaking views of San Francisco's scenic landscape.

I witnessed Sunrun's ascent to become a top leader in the residential solar installation business in the United States during my years of involvement in its strategic sourcing and procurement processes.

Sunrun operates as an innovative business platform that fosters the growth and prosperity of both their own direct installers and carefully selected third-party local or regional installers. Pioneering solar leasing, Sunrun unlocked the vast potential of the residential solar market. Their success can be attributed to their strength in solar financing, substantial purchasing power for solar equipment, streamlined business operations, and, most notably, an open hybrid business model and human-centric company culture.

On the busy streets of San Francisco, SolarCity, with its eye-catching white and green cars adorned with SolarCity logos, caught my attention, and earned a spot on my target customer list.

Elon Musk once said, "That free fusion reactor in the sky (the Sun) conveniently converts ~4 million tons of mass into energy every second. We just need to catch an extremely tiny amount of it to power all of civilization." With its sci-fi-esque name, SolarCity embodied innovation and cutting-edge solar technologies.

SolarCity installed our solar inverters in three states, and I was involved in their strategic sourcing and procurement process. Throughout my collaboration with SolarCity, including leading their factory visits, I witnessed their comprehensive end-to-end business strategies, from solar panel manufacturing, to financing, installation, and after-sales services. At SolarCity, which was later acquired by Tesla, people had the opportunity to participate in almost every aspect of the solar supply chain.

Expand your perspective beyond the individual business, under the guiding light of Enso's Inner House of Business Framework, and delve into the intricacies of the solar industry supply chain.

Take, for instance, solar financing companies. While one may focus solely on financing, another may also offer installation services, covering more supply chain segments. Within each segment of the supply chain, it's crucial to study the unique business models at play. For instance, one solar manufacturer sells directly to installers, while another chose to distribute through solar distributors.

By understanding the unique dynamics of businesses across the supply chain, we can make wise and informed decisions about our business's role in the solar industry.

Now, let's turn to your business.

If you're new to your industry, consider the specific supply chain segment you aspire to be a part of, which is aligned with your genius. Look beyond your immediate environment and seek insights from people who are already immersed in your industry.

If you're employed by a large company, identify how your work in the segment can contribute value to the whole supply chain. Focus on those interconnection aspects and strive for excellence.

If you run a smaller business, strategically choose a business segment within your industry that allows for rapid and profitable growth, and that is aligned with your unique soul seeds. Consider options such as becoming a third-party installer for a top solar company like Sunrun, joining a solar purchasing consortium, or establishing a standalone solar business.

By examining your role within the supply chain of your industry and understanding its broader context, you position yourself for success.

E - Equipment: Unveil Soul of Business

The image of a spotless white inverter in a graceful exhibition space at the solar trade show in Texas is still in my mind after many years. It was the starting point of a decade-long business collaboration with my big client.

A product embodies the soul of the business.

I take a systematic approach to evaluating solar equipment. A solar system comprises various components, including solar panels, inverters, mounting systems, monitoring devices, and accessories, each bearing the names of different brands from manufacturers. Each discipline played a crucial role in shaping the industry.

Within this landscape, I observed a diverse array of professionals bringing their expertise to the table. More chemical engineers delved into the research and development of solar panels, while more mechanical engineers focused on advancing solar racking technologies. More electrical engineers, on the other hand, honed their skills in perfecting solar inverter technologies.

When choosing a business to start or join, I relied on a blend of evaluation and intuition, placing greater emphasis on the merits of its products rather than the business's size or reputation.

However, amidst the abundance of products, certain illusions emerged. It became clear that we needed a guiding light to navigate this complex terrain.

Illusion #1: We place our trust in the peak performance data found in product data sheets.

Peak performance data primarily reflects controlled lab testing results, and field performance, influenced by various real environmental conditions, may deviate from these data points. Thus, the true measure of a product's worth lies in its real-world performance.

Illusion #2: We blindly chase the most advanced technologies in the market.

Technological progress often accompanies a learning curve, during which product flaws are addressed and performance is improved over time. Some technologies may fail to withstand the test of time, underscoring the importance of product reliability.

Illusion #3: We are swayed by the allure of big-name companies alone.

Surprisingly, certain industry giants excel in marketing and sales despite offering average products, while smaller pioneering companies prioritize product excellence at their core. Company size does not always determine product superiority.

A Simple Formula

To simplify the quest for the best solar products, I devised a straightforward formula:

Long-term Performance = Everyday Performance × Uptime

Here, I emphasized that the reliability of solar equipment is just as significant as its everyday performance.

In building a sustainable solar system, we must consider both factors in tandem.

If you are new to the solar industry, reflect on the solar equipment that ignites your imagination and passion. It may be a fitting career path for you.

If you currently work in the realm of solar equipment businesses, contemplate how your contributions interact with other components to deliver the ultimate customer experience through a comprehensive solar system. Expand your knowledge to encompass value-added integrations.

If your work does not directly involve solar equipment, consider how leveraging your understanding of solar equipment can enhance the customer experience. Broaden your knowledge to elevate your market value.

In the realm of solar equipment, where innovation intertwines with practicality, your journey awaits.

S - Standards: Unleash Power of Compliance

In the early days of studying our competitors, an inverter manufacturer with headquarters in Israel was barely a blip on the radar. However, when the Rapid Shutdown Device standards and regulations were introduced in California to mitigate the risk of fires, they recognized the significance of this opportunity. They swiftly designed their products, got certified with the new standards, then emerged as the market leader in the residential solar inverter market in the United States. They have dominated this niche market for years. It was Standards & Regulations that set them apart.

Witnessing this transformation, I learned about the importance of compliance with Standards & Regulations. The design-to-production product life cycle for our Rapid Shutdown Device solution was one of the fastest I had ever seen. The reason was simple: we couldn't sell any inverter products without it. Working closely with top solar standard experts, we designed a unique solution that gained wide acceptance from local jurisdictions and quickly spread our large volume installations nationwide.

Standards & Regulations are far from being mere stacks of documents gathering dust on shelves. They embody stories of growing solar adoptions and seizing opportunities, beyond addressing safety concerns.

Here's another remarkable example. Concerns about solar saturation loomed large in California, putting solar installations on hold and capping the renewable portfolio standards solar goals in the state. Yet, solar energy accounted for only a tiny fraction of the overall energy mix. The true challenge lay with the aging utility grids, struggling to accommodate the influx of distributed solar energy, which disrupted their stability and safety. In response, the IEEE™ networking standard and the SunSpec Common Smart Inverter Profile (CSIP) were introduced alongside California Rule 21. This breakthrough enabled an amazing scale of solar adoption, benefiting all industry participants.

Solar Standards & Regulations encompass a broad spectrum, including IEEE international standards, NEC national electric codes in the United States, SunSpec data communication standards, local jurisdiction standards, and more. Each country has its own sets.

A high-ranking executive from UL, a global safety certification company, shared his insights on the two types of people involved: those who work on the content of standards and regulations as experts, and those who coordinate the efforts of various stakeholders in shaping and implementing these standards.

If you are new to your industry, consider working on the standards and regulations, which can elevate your standing amidst the crowd. Understand and learn them diligently to position yourself as a knowledgeable and valuable professional expert.

If you are already working in Solar, delve into the standards and regulations that directly impact your work. Study them deeply to ensure compliance and stay at the forefront of industry developments to gain a competitive advantage for your business.

If you are engaged in the realm of solar standards and regulations, ponder how you can share your knowledge and assist other solar professionals, collaborating to foster a community of empowered individuals driving the industry standards and regulations forward to improve safety and solar adoptions.

Standards & Regulations are not to be overlooked or underestimated. They hold the potential to shape the trajectory of the solar industry and empower those who embrace them.

T - Transformation: Embrace Your Journey of Growth

I discovered two powerful pathways to personal transformation.

The first path is learning **How to Unlearn**. Yes, you heard it right. It's essential not to cling too tightly to outdated self-limiting beliefs, old habits, obsolete knowledge, old ways of thinking, old identities, etc. Periodically, we must empty what we have learned in the past to create space for fresh and new knowledge.

The second path is learning **How to Learn**. The pandemic and new technologies such as Artificial Intelligence have changed our lives and work, demanding that we adapt and evolve. It is now more important than ever to sharpen our learning skills so we can stay in the driver's seat of our lives.

If you are new to the solar industry, consider how you can co-create the new solar landscape using your imagination, creativity, and intuition. Hone these skills to contribute to the industry's transformation and growth.

If you are already working in Solar, take a moment to find a quiet space, listen to your inner voice, and observe a better version of you that's yearning to emerge—a version capable of uplifting the industry and achieving greater financial success for you and your family, or something even more profound, protecting our Mother Earth.

If you find yourself among the top performers in the industry, consider how you can share your knowledge and expertise with your peers in a non-competitive environment. Teaching others not only benefits them but also enhances your own learning and growth. Embrace the role of a mentor and foster a collaborative atmosphere that nurtures collective success.

Transformation is a continuous process, an ongoing journey of growth and self-discovery. Embrace the courage to unlearn, the passion to learn, and the willingness to share and unlock the limitless possibilities that await you on this remarkable path.

A - Applications: Unlock the Power to Illuminate the World

Picture this: a white solar inverter standing gracefully on the oceanfront after a devastating typhoon. In that moment, I witnessed the beautiful illustration of solar applications. When it comes to ocean-side solar installations, we must carefully select inverters that have withstood rigorous tests for high-pressure water resistance, ensuring no water leakage compromises their integrity. We seek those that have passed salt spray testing, meaning they will endure the corrosive effects of their seaside environment. And, of course, we employ specialized installation techniques tailored to these unique, windy, ocean-side locations.

Amidst the boundless sunshine that graces our planet, why not harness the remarkable potential of solar energy applications to address the Climate Change challenge? This thought sparked an exciting journey for me—one filled with discovery and global collaborations.

Working in the realm of solar energy applications is more than just a job; it's an exhilarating experience that brings together solar professionals from diverse backgrounds, transcending geographical boundaries, and potentially illuminating solar light upon millions of people across the globe.

Now imagine a solar professional living on the western shores of the Pacific Ocean, learning invaluable solar application lessons from someone residing on the opposite side of the globe. In this non-competitive global space, we can share and learn best practices that drive our solar businesses forward. Furthermore, this exchange of knowledge propels the widespread adoption of solar energy across the world, heralding a brighter and more sustainable future for all.

If you are new to solar, which solar applications would

capture your passion? Try to picture these solar applications in the solar roles you will be playing to inspire your imagination and creativity.

Document your solar applications, capturing the essence of your business, covering varieties such as installation environment, customer types, solar equipment etc.

Open yourself up to learning from the best practices in solar applications, not only within your organization or region but from across the globe. Embrace the wealth of knowledge available and apply it to enhance your own endeavors to stand out among competitors.

Share your solar applications, carefully selecting non-confidential information within a collaborative and non-competitive environment. By sharing our triumphs and challenges, we foster an environment of growth and collective progress. Through sharing, we ignite a spark of inspiration that fuels the solar revolution.

F - Financing: Unlock the Potential of Solar Energy

It was a year-long endeavor to secure a coveted spot on the top banks' national approved vendor list. Their meticulous evaluation scrutinized every aspect of our business, from our track record of business performance to the unwavering reliability of our solar equipment, the resilience of our global supply chain, the quality evaluation and assurance system, and the strength of our service support infrastructure. Through this rigorous evaluation process, we cemented our position as a trusted business partner in the solar industry and made our products widely adopted globally. We were one of few on the list.

Through this, I developed a deep appreciation for financing. Financing—often perceived as a realm of dry numbers—transforms into a vibrant catalyst when we understand how it enables people to embrace the benefits of solar energy. Just as the financing manager warmly welcomed me into our local car dealership, unveiling an array of financing options for my vehicle purchase, similar options are available for investing in solar systems. From leasing and power purchase agreements (PPA) to loans and cash purchases, the world of solar financing opens doors to an abundance of mass solar adoptions.

If you are new to the solar industry, envision how you would secure financing for your business and how you would provide flexible financing options to your customers. Explore avenues that ensure businesses thrive in this dynamic field.

If you are already a part of the solar business but not directly involved in financing, take a moment to walk in your customers' shoes. How is your business currently offering financing options to your customers? By understanding their perspectives and needs, you will rapidly expand your knowledge and uncover fresh opportunities for career growth.

If you are actively engaged in solar financing, challenge yourself to evaluate how your offerings are delivered to customers. Sometimes, forging strategic partnerships with solar distributors or integrating into solar design software packages can yield optimal results. Remain attuned to the ever-evolving solar financing landscape and be open to conducting experiments that incorporate the latest and most beneficial financing options into your solar business.

S - Services: Creating Delightful Customer Experiences

In the realm of solar energy, where equipment endures for 20+ years, the true essence lies in the services that accompany it. Service encompasses a commitment to delivering exceptional customer experiences throughout the solar journey.

The rapid advancement of IT has brought traditional services into the modern age. Drawing from my experience as an Accenture management consultant involved in implementing enterprise resource planning (ERP) systems for Fortune 500 global companies, I architected and designed our comprehensive service support infrastructure. It was supported by experienced service engineers, one of the key factors that helped us win top clients and propelled our U.S. business to be recognized as one of the top 10 solar technologies consulting service companies.

If you are new to the solar industry, envision how you could provide the best service to your customers. Write down your ideas for service offerings, map out the roadmap for organizing your service team, explore the digital technical platforms that will streamline your operations, and define the service levels you aim to deliver. By envisioning your unique service strategy, you set the stage for building strong relationships with your customers throughout the lifecycle of products.

If you are already immersed in the solar business, take a moment to contemplate how you upgrade your service support infrastructure, or how your work impacts the services provided to customers. By gaining a deeper understanding of how your role contributes to the overall customer experience, you can uncover opportunities for personal growth.

If you are currently engaged in solar services, seize the

opportunity to explore best practices beyond the confines of the solar industry. Look beyond its youthful industry boundaries and draw inspiration from the exceptional service experiences you have encountered—whether it's purchasing a smartphone, acquiring a PC, or seeking medical care. For example, I designed our RMA product return process, which was inspired by the RMA return and repair experience of my personal computer. Embrace the spirit of experimentation and incorporate the best practices you uncover into your own service offerings.

Business is Art, in Zen Simplicity

"Business is the starry intersection of Science and Art."

– Susanna Huang

A Poem About Starbucks Bears

The little bears came to the shop,
sitting on the coffee beans,
in deep and light shades.

The little bears flew across the Atlantic,
to Africa, the hometown of coffee beans,
sniffing the sweet and bitter tastes,
at the faraway Starbucks place.

– "Moon Creek" Poetry

"PRICE" Flows, Be Water

"Be Water, Business Friends!"

– Susanna Huang

We live in certain systems, like business systems, social systems, ecosystems, the solar system, the milk-way, etc.

In this book, I introduced some of my new Zen-inspired business systems, Enso's Inner House of Business Framework, CATS, SOAK, PACKS, and the 7 Stars Global Solar Education Guide.

I often elevate myself from the daily operations to get a bird's-eye view of the whole industry's supply chain, from the white clouds. I do not like being a frog in the well. Trained rigorously in electrical engineering, I embrace the profound wisdom of intricate big-system thinking.

Having grown up in an ancient city with over 3000 years of history, where the ancient Chinese philosopher Laozi wrote and taught Da De Jing, offering wisdom on the nature of the Dao (the Way), and advocating for a life of simplicity, humility, and harmony, I was deeply influenced by Eastern philosophies.

"Chi" is "visible" in my eyes, flowing through the industry supply chain.

People can get sick when "Chi" is blocked from circulating in some parts of human bodies.

Similarly, businesses can get sick when "Chi" is blocked from circulating in some parts of business areas.

It is important to clear the "Business Chi Pathways" and purify the "Business Chi Flows."

I observed five magical and valuable flows in our businesses, naming them "PRICE".

P – Product Flow
R – Reverse Flow
I - Information Flow
C – Cash Flow
E – Energy Flow

P - Product Flow

Product flow is a journey that starts with producing exceptional products, ensuring their safe transportation, delivering properly at client locations, and using them in various applications.

It flows from a manufacturer (or a service provider) to a customer, providing value in exchange for profits.

We nurture excellence from creation to consumption in the product flow, fine-tuning and improving this intricate process continuously.

R - Reverse Product Flow

The Reverse Product Flow typically refers to the RMA (Return Merchandise Authorization) process, where delivered products are returned by the customer to the manufacturer, with or without product issues as defined in the return policies.

This process covers product diagnosis by our service engineers, remotely or onsite, and the authorized product returns to the warehouse for repairs or scraps.

We designed the Reverse Product Flow process into our customized CRM service platform, where the reports are generated periodically according to the Key Performance Indicators (KPIs) for measurements and continuous improvements.

Sometimes, this process also includes the product scrapping and recycling processes, emphasizing environmental protection.

This Reverse Product Flow process directly impacts customer experience and satisfaction and should not be underestimated.

I - Information Flow

We gather information throughout our entire business organization and during the lifecycle of our products.

In the ever-evolving business landscape, this information guides our business decisions with fresh knowledge, helping us navigate the turbulent waters.

Information flow encompasses both internal communications and external outreach, typically a two-way channel. If the "Chi" of the information flow is blocked, the company's performance in those areas are affected.

First, let's examine whether the internal information flow within the company is smooth.

- Can the entrepreneur make wise decisions at lightning speed, as in the early days of the business?
- Is critical information stuck in the hands of mediocre middle managers?
- Is the information being disrupted by countless inefficient meetings that waste time?
- Is the information getting buried under piles of fancy talk that lacks substance?

Next, let's assess whether the information between the company and the outside world is seamless.

- Is the entrepreneur respected and admired by the ex-

ternal world, as in the early days of the business?
- Is the company's information misunderstood by external business partners?
- Is there an information overload or insufficiency that hinders effective collaborations?
- Is the entrepreneur's information intentionally altered by certain individuals, affecting business brand reputation?

During the rapid growth phase of the company, it is crucial to focus on the genuine flow of internal information and the communications with the outside world.

C - Cash Flow

Imagine we're in the Sahara Desert together. I take a bottle of water and pour it onto the scorching sand, and the water instantly disappears without a trace. Then, I take another bottle of water and pour it onto the scorching sand, and that water also vanishes instantly. I run out of water and ask you, standing beside me, bewildered by my interesting behavior, to give me another bottle of water. I prepare to pour it onto the scorching sand. More often than not, you won't give me another bottle of water.

The water flows out and doesn't come back, serving no purpose.

My "Business Financing Request" is denied by you, illustrated by this fable.

Difficulty in securing financing for our business is a common pain point.

The best cash flow comes from our own sales. Additionally, financing is crucial.

Now, let me tell another fable.

Imagine we're standing on a small oasis in the Sahara Desert, my oasis. I take a bottle of water and pour it onto the vegetation in the oasis, and the water is absorbed by the plants. Then, I take another bottle of water and pour it onto the vegetation in the oasis. The leaves of the plants become greener. I run out of water and ask you, who is standing beside me, to give me some water to preserve this oasis and make it larger and more robust. In the second fable, the product I provide to customers is "a small oasis." This small oasis "locks in" precious water in the desert. I prove that my good product, "a small oasis," can bring value to customers while consuming water efficiently.

Cash flow elevates resources from investment to profit realization.

At this point, financing becomes easier with a proven cash flow projection from our business.

E - Energy Flow

I've long pondered the secret behind Starbucks' extraordinary success in the coffee industry, with my humble entrepreneurial beginnings at a local Starbucks Café, inside a Barnes & Noble bookstore.

Immersing myself in the autobiography of the Starbucks founder, Mr. Schultz, I seem to have found the answer while reflecting on my own experiences at Starbucks. Why would I drive to Starbucks to savor a cup of latte, cappuccino, or mocha, when I have the comfort of home and instant coffee for less than a dollar? Was I merely purchasing a cup of coffee, or was it something more attractive?

Mr. Schultz grew up in a poor neighborhood. His father

had a work-related injury but no health insurance. He vowed to nurture and respect every employee, like his father, in his Starbucks coffee company. Even part-time employees were offered company-provided health insurance, career training, and tuition reimbursement. From caring for the coffee farmers at the cultivation sites to the barista preparing a fragrant cup of Starbucks coffee for me, Kindness, a beautiful energy, flows through Starbucks' global supply chain.

Kindness energy fuels ethical and sustainable business practices.

One can only feel the vibration of the delicate radiance of Kindness energy flow with keen insight.

I often exchange a few words with friendly and fun baristas between immersing myself in work.

Kindness energy has illuminated the Starbucks brand with an indescribable aura of beauty, attracting countless customers like me to become frequent visitors.

Similarly, global companies prioritize those suppliers flowing with kindness energy, not just evaluating their products and services. They also often favor enterprises with sustainable, eco-friendly, low-carbon, and fair labor usage practices.

What attracts customers is not merely tangible products or services, but the intangible Kindness Energy that fosters a delightful emotional experience.

"U & I": The New Rules of Business

"Small and Graceful Business Blooms in Zen Garden of Ultra-Simplicity."

– Susanna Huang

This is the last chapter of this book, but I hope Little Stone Lion inspires a new chapter in your business adventure.

We now walk into a swiftly shifting New World, with unknowns and uncertainties.

Goodbye, dinosaur age. The smaller species survived the mass extinction of dinosaurs and in this new business world, small businesses may survive the mass extinction of business giants.

The relationship between businesses may no longer be like in the animal world, with fierce competitions, a Net-Zero game.

The relationship between businesses might be like flowers and trees, growing alone yet interconnected.

A new rule appears for our new business world:

You and I: U & I – Uniqueness & Interconnectedness.

U – Uniqueness

Each business grows from the soul seed of its founder. It is unique in the Universe, growing gracefully and providing values. It radiates its own beautiful aura of glow, in the vast business forest.

I – Interconnectedness

Businesses, like the flowers and trees in the forest, are interconnected.

We form the fluid network of business ecosystem with our carefully selected business partners.

Each business is unique, a flower grows like a flower, a tree grows like a tree, you are you, I am me.

Our business forms like water, changing shapes with the changing environment.

We form a business ecosystem to provide a total solution across the supply chain.

Each of our businesses in this ecosystem might be small, but graceful and powerful, with mutual respect. Together, we become the long-term business partners of business giants, a few survivors.

Little Stone Lion: The End

"You are also a Lion King inside."

— Susanna Huang

I often walked past this little stone lion in my neighborhood. It reminded me of one of my favorite Disney movies, The Lion King. The courage of the young Lion King is the heart to fight without fear, often seen in the spirits of entrepreneurs.

So, I name this book *Little Stone Lion*.

This book documents my entrepreneurship journey: Go Global. In Zen. In Green.

However, *Little Stone Lion* is not a memoir or traditional business book.

My intention is not just sharing my knowledge, I wanted to help you learn how to apply Enso's Inner House of Business Framework to your business, so you can become a top brand business in your niche market.

I also wanted to share my transformative experience of living life as an experiment, seeking the meaning of life, discovering my true self, solving challenging problems, overcoming fears, and developing courage.

Are you resonating with me across the time and space, right now?

Drawing from what I've shared, you can accelerate your business growth, minimizing the investments and risks, and more importantly, feel fulfilled with inner peace for the business success you will achieve.

You are also ME in this vast benevolent Universe.

We could feel unselfish love in our open hearts,

We could listen to our subtle inner voices,

We could live mindfully in the moment,

We could shine our bright light,

Living in our little corners.

Thank you for joining me on this amazing journey in Joy, Peace, and Harmony, rare in the business world.

You are also a Lion King inside.

About the Author: Rising from Nothingness

"The Cowardly Lion finds Courage in His Own Heart."

— The Wizard of Oz

My inspiration for business started with my dad. My dad was an engineer turned business entrepreneur. He adored me unconditionally. I loved him dearly and respected him hugely. My dream was to become a scholar in business, not do business, to stand next to my dad. Sadly, he passed away before my dream came true. I went on in my life as a management consultant for Fortune 500 companies. But I could feel a big void in my heart where my hero daddy used to reside in bubbling happiness. I could no longer fool my heart.

Looking back, my life in big corporations was comfortable, working on exciting global digital transformation projects and large and complex strategic sourcing initiatives for some of the world's most influential Fortune 500 companies.

However, I walked into business following my dad's footprints, and I naively thought I would feel him there. My Green Energy Village LLC, a boutique management consulting business, was founded in 2011 with nothing more than a laptop and a vision in our local Starbucks Café in a Barnes & Noble bookstore.

But I didn't know I was walking on an untraveled entrepreneurship road. This solar business brought me to many places in the world, seeing many faces—happy or worried, and hearing many voices—kind or jealous.

My seeking led to a different, unexpected path. I was indeed walking my own path, not my dad's path. I was in constant self-doubt, but I never stopped.

Years later, my dedication and expertise have grown my business to be a multi-million-dollar company, and it is a woman-owned, minority-owned business built by an immigrant. We earned the prestigious honor of winning the top solar brand award, and were nominated as a top 10 solar technologies consulting service company in the United States.

A small and graceful business earned its unique space

among business giants.

"Enso's Inner House of Business Framework" surfaced when I wrote this book.

I had a unique 360-degree business experience that spans start-up and established businesses, both large and small, in marketing, sales, and product and service operations across the Eastern and Western world — Going Global, in Zen and In Green.

Since everyone is familiar with a house, I use this metaphor to illustrate my business philosophies—Enso's Inner House of Business Framework—so you will easily understand.

Unlike other business frameworks in the marketplace, my work is also influenced by years of Zen Meditation practice. This business framework is ultra-simple for you to quickly apply to your business, holistically and systematically. It comes directly from my experience of solving real-world business problems in a rapidly changing environment of the fast-growing industry, with sparks of business intuition.

This management philosophy of melding Eastern and Western thinking could help entrepreneurs build profitable businesses cost effectively, while developing long-lasting top brands in niche markets. It will bring out your inner wisdom for best decision-making and mitigate business risks.

Kazuo Inamori was a Japanese entrepreneur and philanthropist, best known as the founder of the Kyocera Corporation and KDDI Corporation, two global Fortune 500 companies. In his book, "Heart," penned when he was nearly 90 years old, he emphasized the following:

The civilization built by humankind is at a pivotal juncture.

From now on, our civilization will transform to make others happier and society better, based on altruism:

- All achievements find their roots in serving others.

- The foremost purpose of life lies in the cultivation of the heart.
- The essence of the heart resonates with the Universe.

A heart of purity and beauty offers three enchanting experiences:
- First, seeing the beautiful dreams painted in your heart being manifested into reality.
- Second, hearing the "whispers of spirits," accomplishing tasks once deemed insurmountable.
- Third, climbing the most challenging cliffs, protected by the miraculous forces of the Universe.

Little Stone Lion is not a traditional business book. It is also me, an entrepreneur full of curiosity, imagination, and a bit of courage, exploring my life purpose in this magical world. Thanks for taking a journey with me into the inner world of *Little Stone Lion* in the tranquil green. I hope you enjoy my personal stories, inspirational or lessons learned.

May the wisdom and knowledge found within these pages be a beam of sunshine to brighten the lives of all who read it.

Acknowledgement

Writing Little Stone Lion has been an amazing journey of reflection, growth, and collaboration, and I am deeply grateful to all those who have supported me along the way.

To my Father, for your love — thank you for being my constant source of strength. To my Daughter, for your talented illustration of Enso's Inner House of Business Framework.

To my mentors, colleagues, and clients, especially those at Accenture and Ginlong Solis, who have shaped my understanding of business and leadership.

A special thanks to Marci Shimoff for your invaluable endorsement and encouragement; your words illuminated this process.

Finally, to my readers—thank you for allowing Little Stone Lion to become a part of your journey. May this book inspire you to pursue your dreams with purpose and to shape businesses that reflect your values.

With gratitude,
Susanna Qiang Huang

www.ingramcontent.com/pod-product-compliance
Lightning Source LLC
Chambersburg PA
CBHW031626160426
43196CB00006B/299